Hugo Iltis

Race, Genetics, and Science:
Resisting Racism in the 1930s

D1602473

1927.

Hugo Iltis (1882–1952) at work in Brno, Czechoslovakia, 1927

Hugo Iltis

Race, Genetics, and Science:
Resisting Racism in the 1930s

•

Foreword by Ondřej Dostál
Director, Mendel Museum, Brno, Czechoslovakia

Introduction by Paul Weindling
Professor, Oxford Brookes University, Oxford England

Translations by
Kareem James Abu-Zeid and Christopher Reid

MASARYK UNIVERSITY
BRNO, CZECH REPUBLIC

2017

Popular Race Theory
Hugo Iltis
Translated from the German by Christopher W. Reid, PhD
German edition: *Volkstümliche Rassenkunde*
"Urania"-Verlagsgesellschaft M.B.H., Jena, 1930

Race in Science and Politics
Hugo Iltis
Translated from the German by Kareem James Abu-Zeid, PhD
German edition: *Rasse in Wissenschaft und Politik*
Prague: Wahrheit, 1935

The Myth of Blood and Race
Hugo Iltis
Translated from the German by Kareem James Abu-Zeid, PhD
German edition: *Der Mythus von Blut und Rasse*
Vienna: Rudolf Harrand Press, 1936
German book cover designed by Hans Waloschek

Translation published by permission of the estate of Hugo Iltis

ISBN 978-80-210-8764-4

CONTENTS

PREFACE

Late in the fall of 1938, Hugo Iltis (1882–1952)[1], Professor of Biology and founder of the Masaryk *Volkshochschule* (People's University)[2] in Brno (Brünn), Czechoslovakia; author of *The Life of Mendel* (1924, translation 1932)[3]; and fiery critic of Nazi racial theories boarded the last flight to England out of Prague's international airport. Aware that the Nazis had read his writings and threatened to string him up in the public square, Iltis feared for his life. By March of 1939 the Germans had stormed into Czechoslovakia and taken it over.

Aided by a letter from Albert Einstein (see below), and with the help of the "Emergency Committee for Displaced German Scholars," Hugo Iltis was one of the lucky academic scientists who escaped capture and imprisonment by the Nazis. His 1936 booklet, *The Myth of Blood and Race* (translated here)[4], had caught the attention of Einstein, who wrote to Iltis on 5 December 1936 from his study at Princeton, stating: "I read your booklet, 'The Myth of Blood and Race,' with great interest and approval. If the majority of the German intellectuals would

---

1 On Hugo Iltis, see https://en.wikipedia.org/wiki/Hugo_Iltis. Iltis received his Ph.D. in Botany at the University of Prague in 1905 after studying biology and botany at the University of Zurich in Switzerland from 1900–1903. In 1906 he became secretary for the Brno society through which Mendel's papers were published (the *Naturforschender Verein*). For a list of Hugo Iltis's papers, see "Hugo Iltis" in Wikipedia.

2 Named after Tomáš Garrigue Masaryk (1850–1937), first president of the newly independent Republic of Czechoslovakia (founded in 1918). Masaryk University (which still exists today) was founded in Brno in 1919. Iltis founded and was director of the separately existing Masaryk People's University (an evening school for adults) from 1921–1938.

3 Hugo Iltis, *Gregor Johann Mendel: Leben, Werk und Wirkung* (Berlin: J. Springer, 1924); Hugo Iltis, *Life of Mendel*, English translation by Eden and Cedar Paul (London: Allen and Unwin, 1932; New York: W. W. Norton, 1932).

4 Hugo Iltis, *Der Mythus von Blut und Rasse* (Vienna: R. Harand, 1936), translated by Kareem James Abu-Zeid as "The Myth of Blood and Race," see this volume.

have shown as much courage and respect for the truth and such a vivid social conscience as the author of this book, the whole nation would have been saved from plunging into such an abyss." Einstein sent a copy of the booklet to W. W. Norton, Iltis's publishing house in New York City, suggesting they print an English translation.[5]

On 4 April 1938, Einstein, who had fled from Germany to the U.S. in 1933, wrote to Iltis urging him to leave Czechoslovakia. "I think you should come first yourself instead of sending your wife in advance," he wrote, "for it certainly would not be of any help should she get a job in a household. You should use your scientific connections to obtain a temporary invitation as a paid lecturer, and then use your presence in this country to attain a permanent appointment."[6]

Einstein then took matters into his own hands. In a letter dated 23 April 1938 to anthropologist Franz Boas at Columbia University (translated in this volume), he wrote: "In such troubled times as these, in which all men of influence are deluged with letters and appeals for help, it pains me doubly to annoy you with the affairs of a single man. In the case of Professor Iltis of Brno, however, I must make an exception." "It is our duty," Einstein said, "to do everything in our power to save this man, while there is still time."[7] With Einstein's support and

---

5   For excerpts from letters from Einstein to Hugo Iltis, originally in possession of his son, Hugh Iltis, Madison, Wisconsin, see https://www.ha.com/heritage-auctions-press-releases-and-news/einstein-letters-to-hugo-iltis-courageous-defier-of-the-nazi-regime-featured-in-dallas-manuscripts-auction.s?releaseId=1834. In *The Myth of Blood and Race*, Iltis had written: "The man who today counts as the most illustrious representative of German science in the entire world, the brilliant mathematician and transformer of the astronomical worldview, Albert Einstein [1879–1955], has been ostracized and exiled from Hitler's Germany, stripped of his honors, and robbed of his possessions" (see this volume). Note: Iltis's *Myth of Blood and Race* was neither translated nor published by W.W. Norton.

6   Einstein to Hugo Iltis, ibid.

7   Einstein to Franz Boas, Image in "Collections of the American Philosophical Society," Philadelphia, PA: https://amphilsoc.org/exhibits/treasures/einstein.htm. Accessed Dec. 1, 2016. Original German in The Hebrew University, Jerusalem, Israel, Albert Einstein archives: http://alberteinstein.info/vufind1/Record/EAR000036839/Copyright#tabnav; "In dieser Zeit allge-

Boas's assistance in arranging a position in the U.S., Hugo Iltis flew to England in December 1938 and within a few weeks traveled on to France.

In January 1939, Iltis's wife and two sons followed him out of Czechoslovakia on a dark train through Germany, with the terrified occupants only pretending to be asleep.[8] A cheer went up as they crossed the border into France. On reaching Cherbourg, Hugo was waving from the top deck of the ship Aquitania and they sailed to New York City. A position agreed upon in advance through Peter Ray Ogden at the International School in Fredericksburg, Virginia, allowed the family to emigrate. This appointment was soon followed by a professorship offered by Edward Alvey, Dean of Fredericksburg's Mary Washington College, and Iltis began a new career as Professor of Biology at Mary Washington.

Race and Genetics

An enthusiastic follower of Gregor Mendel's experimental work on the breeding of peas that had established the science of genetics, Iltis had gathered many materials on Mendel in Brno, where he raised funds to construct a Mendel monument in 1910 now in the Monastery courtyard, wrote his biography of Mendel (*Gregor Johann Mendel: Leben, Werk und Wirkung* 1924; English translation 1932), and founded the Mendel Museum in 1932.

In the preface to his biography of Mendel, Iltis wrote: "Few publications have so enduringly and variously influenced science as has the short monograph by the Augustinian monk of Brünn, Pater Gregor Mendel. Forgotten for decades, within a few years after its rediscovery it gave a mighty impetus to the doctrine of heredity; and as Mendelism, his teaching has now become the central theme of biological research as well as the foundation of manifold practical applications." Iltis went on to relate that as a schoolboy he had

meiner Bedrängnis, in der alle einflussreichen," Archive #53–502. © The Hebrew University of Jerusalem. Printed by permission. See translation by Kareem Abu Zeid in this volume.

8   Anni Liebscher Iltis (1900–1987); Wilfred (Fred) Gregor Iltis (1923–2008); Hugh Hellmut Iltis (1925–2016). Anni Iltis helped Hugo to think through his ideas and edit his manuscripts.

actually read Mendel's original paper in the museum library in Brno before it was rediscovered, but did not grasp its significance at the time. When Mendel's work became famous, Iltis—a university student at the time—decided to gather as much information from family, friends, and other sources as possible. Based on this research and his work in Brno, Iltis published numerous papers on Mendel, ultimately culminating in his 1924 biography.[9]

It was Iltis's understanding of genetics, gained both as a scientist and through his papers and book on Mendel, that buttressed his instincts that the Nazis were going beyond the evidence and using genetics in an ideological manner. Nazi writings held that the Aryan Germanic peoples were superior to the Jews intellectually, culturally, and physically. Through breeding, the blood of inferior types such as Jews and Slavs, the Nazis argued, would contaminate the blood of Germanic and other Nordic peoples. The purity of the blood of the "master race" should be preserved though controlled breeding (eugenics), while inferior races should be eliminated through sterilization and extermination. To Iltis, these ideas constituted "intellectual poison gas."[10]

---

9   In 1900, Mendel's work was rediscovered by Hugo de Vries, Carl Correns, and Eric von Tschermak (https://en.wikipedia.org/wiki/History_of_genetics). On Iltis's reading of Mendel's paper as a schoolboy, see Iltis, *Gregor Johann Mendel: Leben, Werk und Wirkung*, "Vorwort," 1924, pp. v-vii and Iltis, *Life of Mendel*, Preface, pp. 9–11, 302, 303. On Iltis's early papers on Mendel, see his *Life of Mendel*, "Preface," footnote 1, p. 9.

10   On the history of Nazi race theory, see https://en.wikipedia.org/wiki/Racial_policy_of_Nazi_Germany. On Hugo Iltis's term "intellectual poison gas," see Iltis (as Bodansky) in *Rasse in Wissenschaft und Politik* (1935), translated by Kareem James Abu Zeid as *Race in Science and Politics*, in this volume, and Iltis, *Myth of Blood and Race*, 1936, Foreword, trans. Abu Zeid, in this volume. In the early decades of the twentieth century discussions occurred over whether Mendelian genetics and Lamarckian eugenics (the inheritance of acquired characteristics) might each have validity. According to Paul Weindling in Marius Turda and Paul Weindling, eds., *Blood and Homeland: Eugenics and Racial Nationalism in Central and Southeast Europe, 1900–1940* (Budapest and New York: Central European Press, 2007), Hugo Iltis did accept certain aspects of Lamarckism (pp. 161, 271). But "Iltis's critique of Nazi race theory as unscientific grew out of his commitment to Mendelism. . . ." (p. 273) His book *Popular Race Theory* (1930, excerpted in this volume) was "targeted at the racial theorist Hans F. K. Günther," condemning him as

Iltis, a Jew who was of German descent and who lived and worked among Slavic peoples in Brno, Czechoslovakia, began to expose the "pseudoscience" behind Nazi thinking. He used his knowledge of genetics and his belief in the equality of all humans to undermine the concept of a superior race. In his *Myth of Blood and Race*, he criticized "the movement from objective race research to blind, fanatical racism" and wrote that "all attempts at providing a scientific foundation to German racism have failed miserably." His writings presented a powerful intellectual critique of the political uses of science by some human beings to discriminate against other human beings. "The different races within a body of people can be compared to the voices in an orchestra," he wrote, "the richer the mixture, or the more polyphonic the melody, the richer the culture will be."[11]

Background of Hugo Iltis's Anti-Racist Theories

How do the ideas of Hugo Iltis on race and genetics fit into the context of his time? And where do they stand in light of subsequent developments? The racism against which Hugo Iltis wrote so forcefully in *The Myth of Blood and Race* (1936) was linked to a concept of blood used in the late 19th and early 20th centuries. Blood was that part of the human body inherited by children and hence by members of families as kinship units.[12]

"unscientific and politically dangerous." Weindling writes that Iltis anticipated the "ominous possibilities of extermination policies" and "rejected the notion of the degenerative effects of racial interbreeding as a political falsehood" (pp. 270–271; see also p. 273 on Nazi "intellectual poison gas"). For more on Iltis and Lamarckism, see Loren Graham, "Attitudes Towards Eugenics in Germany and Soviet Russia in the 1920s: An Examination of Science and Values," in Daniel Callahan and H. Tristram Englehardt, Jr., eds., *The Roots of Ethics: Science, Religion, and Values* (New York: Plenum Press, 1976), pp. 339–369, see esp. pp. 344–345.

11 For quotations, see Iltis, *The Myth of Blood and Race*, translated in this volume.

12 *Oxford English Dictionary*, s.v., "blood," III: "Race and kindred as connoted by blood," 8. "Blood is popularly treated as the typical part of the body which children inherit from their parents and ancestors; hence that of parents and children, and of the members of a family or race, is spoken of as identical, and as being distinct from that of other families or races."

Racists held that some bloodlines were superior to others. "Superior" peoples could supposedly maintain their supremacy by not interbreeding with "inferior" peoples. The field of eugenics, as formulated by Francis Galton (1822–1911) in his books *Hereditary Genius* (1869) and *Inquiries into Human Faculty and Its Development* (1883), maintained that the human population could be improved by controlled breeding. Nazi propaganda held that the Nordic (Aryan) race was superior to all other races and that Germanic peoples should maintain that superiority by controlling or eliminating inferior races, especially people of Jewish descent. Other researchers argued that physiological characteristics such as skin color and skull shape could be used to show that "colored" races were most closely linked to apes and were therefore inferior to whites. On the basis of craniological studies, several scientists maintained that negro skull shapes were only a step up from those of apes and were inferior to the skulls of whites, especially whites of Greco-Roman descent. Such studies led to racial segregation and compulsory sterilization as a means of preventing whites from cross-breeding with inferior races, and also led to racial hygiene as a means of preserving higher mental faculties among whites.[13]

In *The Myth of Blood and Race* (see this volume), Iltis stated bluntly that "We know that the German people represent a thoroughly hybrid racial mixture; we know that much greater racial differences can arise among non-Jewish Germans than between Germans and Jews; and we know that the concept 'German blood' is a fantastical entity that does not correspond to anything in reality." He quoted the "Special Provisions for Jews" in the "Law on Nationality and Reich Citizenship" that stated: "Marriages between Jews and citizens of German or related blood are forbidden." All violators would be imprisoned. But, Iltis countered forcefully, "There is no Aryan race, there is no "German or related blood." "The German race laws through which the Jews are abused are built on lies. And racism, the worldview of the Nazis, is also built on lies."[14]

---

13 Francis Galton, *Hereditary Genius* (New York: D. Appleton, 1881, originally published 1869); Galton, *Inquiries into Human Faculty and Its Development* (London: MacMillan,1883); "Scientific Racism," https://en.wikipedia.org/wiki/Scientific_racism.

14 Iltis, *The Myth of Blood and Race*, see this volume.

In his *Myth of Blood and Race*, Hugo Iltis was especially critical of the theories of Arthur de Gobineau (1816–1882), Hans Günther (1891–1968), and Eugen Fischer (1874–1967), all of whom influenced Hitler and were revered by the Nazis. In his *Essay on the Inequality of the Human Races* (1853–1855), French writer Arthur de Gobineau argued that there were three human races: white, black, and yellow. Whites were subdivided, with the Aryan (later Nordic) race in France being superior to non-Aryans. Interbreeding would lead to the deterioration of humankind. Gobineau tried to prove, Iltis wrote, "that all progress, all genuine culture was thanks solely to the 'Aryan' race, who laid down laws as the master and conqueror of the world." Gobineau had "abandoned the foundation of objective representation free of hatred or favoritism and introduced the disastrous method of evaluating races."[15]

Hans F.K. Günther in his *Racial Science of the German People* (*Rassenkunde des deutschen Volkes*, 1922) argued that the Germanic, Nordic (or Aryan) people were the noblest and most intellectually creative of all peoples and were superior to other races, while the Jews were the lowest. The Aryan race could be improved through breeding with superior peoples. Gunther's ideas were the backbone of Hitler's racism and Nazi propaganda. In *The Myth of Blood and Race*, Iltis called Günther the "race messiah" and stated, "Whoever has read Günther is ripe for the reading of *Mein Kampf*!"[16]

---

15 "Arthur de Gobineau," https://en.wikipedia.org/wiki/Arthur_de_Gobineau; Gobineau, *The Moral and Intellectual Diversity of Races* (J.B. Lippincott, 1856); Gobineau, *The Inequality of Human Races* (G.P. Putnam's Sons, 1915). Quotation in Hugo Iltis, *The Myth of Blood and Race*, translated in this volume.

16 Hans F. K. Günther, https://en.wikipedia.org/wiki/Hans_F._K._ Günther. Günther, *Rassenkunde des deutschen Volkes* (München, J.F. Lehmann, 1922); Günther, *The Racial Elements of European History*, trans. G. C. Wheeler (London: Methuen, 1927). Iltis wrote: "Günther has a very skillful method of racist propaganda. From somewhat arbitrarily chosen photographs, he constructs not only the races but also the different racial strains. As examples for the 'agreeable' races, and particularly for the Nordic race, he selects beautiful heads with elegantly done hair from the upper classes of society; for the 'disagreeable' races, e.g., the Alpine or Jewish races, the selection is less favorable." See Hugo Iltis, *The Myth of Blood and Race*, translated in this volume.

Eugen Fischer, professor of anthropology at Freiburg University in Germany, promoted Günther's ideas. Fischer wrote *The Rehoboth Bastards and the Problem of Miscegenation among Humans* (1913) and *Principles of German Heredity and Race Hygiene* in 1921. In the *Rehoboth Bastards*, he studied the Basters (from whom the word bastard is derived), who were children of German (Boer) men and native (Hottentot) women in Namibia, Africa. Fischer's arguments that they not be allowed to reproduce led to the prohibition of interracial marriages in the German colonies. He also measured the skulls and took blood from blacks and gypsies in Germany, studied bones and skeletons, and conducted experiments on Jews. In 1927, he was appointed Director of the Kaiser Wilhelm Institute of Anthropology, Human Heredity, and Eugenics in Berlin, and in 1933 signed the "Loyalty Oath of German Professors to Adolph Hitler and the Nationalist Socialist State." In 1927, Fischer and Günther co-authored a book on German heads of the Nordic Race with images (*Deutsche Köpfe nordischer Rasse: 50 Abbildungen mit Geleitwarten*). In *The Myth of Blood and Race*, Iltis wrote: "Eugen Fischer, today's leader of the racists, was once a highly regarded researcher." Fischer's own research, Iltis argued, contradicted his racist lies.[17]

The racist theories of German Nazis were countered by anthropologists Franz Boas (1858–1942) and Ruth Benedict (1887–1948). Boas, who developed cultural

---

17 Eugen Fischer, https://en.wikipedia.org/wiki/Eugen_Fischer. Fischer, *The Rehoboth Bastards and the Problem of Miscegenation among Humans* (1913) (*Die Rehobother Bastards und das Bastardierungsproblem beim Menschen: anthropologische und ethnographische Studien am Rehobother Bastardvolk in Deutsch-Südwest-Afrika*) Eugen Fischer and H.F.K. Günther. *Deutsche Köpfe nordischer Rasse: 50 Abbildungen mit Geleitwarten* (Munich: J.F. Lehmann. 1927). On the Rehoboth Basters of Namibia (from whom the word 'bastard' is derived), see https://en.wikipedia.org/wiki/Baster and http://wikivisually.com/wiki/Eugen_Fischer. Paul Weindling, see "Introduction" to this volume, states that Iltis "was prepared to seriously engage with and partly to accept the work of the Eugen Fischer, although he remained critical of his linking psychological to physical types." In *The Myth of Blood and Race*, Iltis stated that Fischer's own research implied that the population of Germany was highly diverse, contradicting his racist ideas. Iltis wrote: "In his famous work *The Rehoboth Basters*, he investigated the variability of the hybrid population that emerged due to the crossbreeding of Dutch people and Hottentots—and came to the conclusion that the population of Germany is every bit as diverse as that hybrid population."

anthropology at Columbia University, worked to protect scholars who were critical of Nazi ideas. Boas argued that ideas of racial inequality were social and not biological and that white and black Americans were equal. Invited by historian W.E.B. Du Bois (1868–1963) of Atlanta University in 1906, Boas gave an address against racism. In 1907, he published an article titled, "Anthropology" in which he stated, "we are interested in the diversity of . . . traits in groups of men found in different geographical areas and in different social classes." Whites had an obligation to argue against racial superiority and to denounce racism. It was through Einstein's letter to Boas that Hugo Iltis received a position in the United States and was able to escape from Czechoslovakia just before the Nazi takeover (see above). In 1943, Boas's student Ruth Benedict, with her female colleague Gene Weltfish, wrote a pamphlet titled, "The Races of Mankind." In it they stated, "[A]ll the peoples of the earth are a single family and have a common origin. We all have just so many teeth, so many molars, just so many little bones and muscles—so we can only have come from one set of ancestors no matter what our color, the shape of our head, the texture of our hair."[18]

In contrast to blood theories of inheritance and the maintenance of racial superiority through racial hygiene, modern genetics holds that genetic variation arose from chance mutations leading to genetic diversity. Genes are redistributed through sexual reproduction. Variation in phenotypic traits—such as skin color, hair quality, skull shape, and facial appearance—can be from genetic adaptations to differing environments selected over long periods of time, individual response to the environment, migration, or chance genetic drift. [19]

Indeed, both scientists and social scientists have argued that the concept of "race" in humans is a perception—a social construct imposed by culture on people's appearance. In the early 20th century W.E.B. Du Bois used biological

---

18 On Franz Boas, see https://en.wikipedia.org/wiki/Franz_Boas. On W.E.B Du Bois, see https://en.wikipedia.org/wiki/W._E._B._Du_Bois. Ruth Benedict and Gene Weltfish, "*The Races of Mankind*," Public Affairs Pamphlet No. 85. New York: Public Affairs Committee, Inc., 1943; https://en.wikipedia.org/wiki/Ruth_Benedict and https://en.wikipedia.org/wiki/Gene_Weltfish.

19 "Race and Genetics," https://en.wikipedia.org/wiki/Race_and_genetics.

and social science to argue that race was not a scientific category and that differences between blacks and whites regarding health were based on social inequalities. Theodosius Dobzhansky (1900–1975) in the 1930s said that the main problem was the misuse of science.[20]

By the 1940s, genes were being studied for their physical characteristics. DNA (deoxyribonucleic acid) was identified as hereditary material in the mid-1940s. The structure of DNA as a double helix was elucidated in the 1950s by Rosalind Franklin, Maurice Wilkins, James Watson, and Francis Crick. Modern genetics has shown that humans are remarkably similar, differing in less than 0.1% of their DNA. And, human DNA is far more variable within human populations, rather than between populations, with 85-90% of the variation found within populations. But, "although many concepts of race are correlated with geographic ancestry, the two are not interchangeable."[21]

Yet the sequencing of the human genome, in the early 2000s, again raised the question of whether people of different continental origins have different DNA and are therefore of different "racial" origins. "Fortunately, modern human genetics can deliver the salutary message that human populations share most of their genetic variation and there is no scientific support for the concept that human populations are discrete, nonoverlapping entities. . . . Thus, genetics can and should be an important tool in helping to both illuminate and defuse the race issue."[22]

---

20 Michael Yudell, Dorothy Roberts, Rob DeSalle, and Sarah Tishkoff, "Taking Race out of Human Genetics," *Science* 351, no. 6273 (Feb. 5, 2016): 564–565; Megan Gannon, "Race is a Social Construct, Scientists Argue," *Scientific American* (Feb 5, 2016); Sheldon Krimsky and Kathleen Sloan, eds., *Race and the Genetic Revolution: Science, Myth, and Culture* (New York: Columbia University Press, 2011).

21 https://geneticshistory.wordpress.com/dnarna-era-1940s-1950/; see also James Watson and Francis Crick, "A Structure for Deoxyribose Nucleic Acid," *Nature* (April 25, 1953); James Watson, *The Double Helix* (New York: Atheneum, 1968); Anne Sayre, *Rosalind Franklin and DNA* (New York: WW Norton, 1975). Witherspoon et al, *Genetics*, 2007 May; 176(1): 351–359, quotation.

22 Jorde and Wooding, 2004 http://www.nature.com/articles/ng1435, quotation. See also Amy Harmon, "In DNA Era New Worries about Prejudice," *New York Times*, Nov. 11, 2007.

According to the 2017 AAPA statement on Race and Equality, "The peoples of the world today appear to possess equal biological potential for assimilating any human culture. Racist political doctrines find no foundation in scientific knowledge concerning modern or past human populations." Also Henry Louis Gates Jr. of Harvard University, director of the W.E.B. Du Bois Institute of African and African American Research, states, "we are walking a fine line between using biology and allowing it to be abused."[23] Gates's argument against using science as the basis for political decisions echoes that made by Hugo Iltis in the 1930s.

Hugo Iltis's Racial Equality

Hugo Iltis's deep engagement with the plant breeding work of Mendel influenced his approach to racial equality. In *The Myth of Blood and Race*, he wrote: "the research of the friar from Brno, Gregor Mendel . . . laid the foundation for a theory that asserted the immutability of hereditary factors, their inability to be altered by external conditions." Iltis exposed the false use of Mendel's work "to support the view that there are by nature higher and lower races . . . ," arguing that "the principle of the purity of races belongs in the world of fairy tales." "We are not against myths and fairy tales," Iltis proclaimed, "it would impoverish humanity if these flowers were to spoil under the icy breath of reason. But making myths and fairy tales the foundation of political action is as dangerous as it is reprehensible."[24]

Iltis's characterizations of Gregor Mendel and Booker T. Washington exemplify the author's commitment to the social and intellectual equality of all humans. Of Booker T. Washington, he wrote: "Personalities such as the Negro leader Booker T. Washington [1856–1915], among others, must convince all who

---

23 AAPA © 2017, quotation from: http://physanth.org/about/position-statements/biological-aspects-race/; Gates quotation, ibid, *New York Times*.

24 Iltis, *Myth of Blood and Race*, quotations from the English translation in this volume.

attempt to deny higher intelligence to the black race that this is not the case."[25] Both of these individuals stand for alternatives to racism and for the equality of all peoples of the world. Together they epitomize Hugo Iltis's intellectual commitment and enduring legacy.

Acknowledgments

It is with deepest gratitude that we acknowledge the translators of Hugo Iltis's writings on "Race, Genetics, and Science." Christopher Reid translated the 1930 pamphlet by Hugo Iltis titled, "Popular Race Theory (*Volkstümliche Rassenkunde*), excerpts from which are published here.[26] Kareem James Abu-Zeid translated the 1935 excerpts from "Race in Science and Politics" (*Rasse in Wissenschaft und Politik*), the 1936 pamphlet, "The Myth of Blood and Race" (*Der Mythus von Blut und Rasse*), and Einstein's letter to Franz Boas (all of which appear in this volume).[27] Both translators have skillfully engaged with the many historical terms and concepts employed in the 1930s that Iltis used to substantiate his theories and clarify his ideas. We thank Carolyn Merchant of the University of California at Berkeley for arranging for the translations, for the structure of the book, for the above preface, and for shepherding it through the production process. We are grateful to biologist Stuart A. Newman of the New York Medical College and to David Iltis for clarification on scientific terms and processes and cautions about the limits of the genetics of Iltis's time.

We are delighted that Paul Weindling, Professor of History, Philosophy, and Religion at Oxford Brookes University, Oxford England, agreed to write the "Introduction," setting Iltis's writings in the context of eugenics, race, and

---

25 Iltis, *Myth of Blood and Race*, quotation from the English translation in this volume.

26 Hugo Iltis, *Volkstümliche Rassenkunde*, English translation by Christopher Reid as "Popular Race Theory" (Jena: Urania-Verlagsgesellschaft, 1930), see this volume.

27 Hugo Iltis, *Rasse in Wissenschaft und Politik*, excerpts translated by Kareem James Abu-Zeid as "Race in Science and Politics" (Prague: Wahrheit, 1935), see this volume. Einstein to Boas, see this volume and note 7 above.

politics during the period leading up to World War II. Weindling is the author and editor of numerous books, among them (with Marius Turda) *Blood and Homeland: Eugenics in Central Europe 1900-1940*, which contains a section devoted to Hugo Iltis.[28]

We likewise appreciate the assistance of Robin Rider, Curator of Special Collections and Department Head at the Memorial Library, University of Wisconsin, Madison, who set up the archive and catalog of Hugo Iltis's papers and made many of them available in digital format. Many other papers and notes, along with some 30 volumes of Hugo Iltis's diaries, are in the Madison collection. Other papers can be found in the Iltis Mendeliana Collection at the University of Illinois Archives.

We are especially grateful to Ondřej Dostál, current Director of the Mendel Museum in Brno that Hugo Iltis founded and Chair of the Association of Museums and Galleries of the Czech Republic, for writing the foreword and for his assistance in publishing this book through the Masaryk University Press in Brno. Of the three essays in this volume, the first essay, "Popular Race Theory," is excerpted in order to avoid duplication. The second, "Race in Science and Politics," which Iltis edited contains the two selections by him (one under the pseudonym Bodansky). The third essay, "The Myth of Blood and Race" is complete.

It was Hugo Iltis's courage, his unflagging dedication to educating ordinary people, and his ability to apply scientific knowledge to exposing Nazi racial theories that led to the writings translated in this book. Today in the Oak Hill Cemetery in Fredericksburg, Virginia, inscribed on the gravestone of Hugo Iltis, are the words—Light to the People; Peace in the World—his motto for the Mazaryk People's University (*Masaryk Volkshochschule*) that he founded in Brno, Czechoslovakia, in 1921.

Most of all we appreciate the scholarship and immense courage displayed by Hugo Iltis in a time of extreme turmoil leading up to World War II.

The Iltis family
Frank, Michael, David, and John Iltis

---

28   On Hugo Iltis, see Turda and Weindling, eds., *Blood and Homeland*, op. cit., note 10, pp. 270–276, 279.

Hugo Iltis Gravestone, Oak Hill Cemetery, Fredericksburg, Virginia

LETTER FROM ALBERT EINSTEIN TO FRANZ BOAS

REGARDING HUGO ILTIS, APRIL 23, 1938[1]

April 23, 1938

Professor Franz Boas
Columbia University
New York City

Dear Professor Boas,

In this time of general distress in which all influential people are so inundated with letters and cries for help, I find it twice as hard to bother you with the affairs of a single individual. In the case of Professor Iltis in Brno, however, I have to make an exception.

Professor Iltis is a biologist, as you can see from the enclosed list of publications. He has become "politically charged" since he allowed a small polemic against the swindle of German racial mysticism to be published, and the present situation means that his life is no longer safe in Czechoslovakia. I believe it is our duty to do everything in our power to save this man, while there is still time. This could be done by providing him with an invitation to give lectures at local universities, in order to enable him to make a start in this country. The enclosed letter from Dr. Walter provides more detailed information about the topics on which Professor Iltis could give lectures.

---

1   English translation by Kareem James Abu Zeid from German original in http://alberteinstein. info/vufind1/Record/EAR000036839/Copyright#tabnav. © The Hebrew University of Jerusalem.

I will also encourage Professor Conklin,[2] a sympathetic and liberal man, to take an interest in Herr Iltis; Herr Conclin [sic] will be returning to Princeton in one week. Since I am not in the department, it is of course not possible for me to directly intervene on behalf of Herr Iltis. But on your advice, I am very ready to do everything that you consider to be correct. Even if you are not able to undertake anything directly, I would be grateful to you for counsel, since I am very interested in safeguarding this man, whom I do not know personally.

With great respect and kind regards,
Yours,

A. Einstein

PS I request the return of Dr. Walter's letter at your convenience.

---

2   Translator's note: Edwin Grant Conklin (1863–1952), who was head of the Biology Department at Princeton University for many years.

FOREWORD

HUGO ILTIS—EDUCATOR, CRITIC, ACTIVIST

Brno: the birthplace of Hugo Iltis. A city which gave the world the genetics of Gregor Mendel. A city seemingly born for innovation and science. As a multicultural city, Brno (in today's Czech Republic) was, until the outbreak of World War II, home to a unique symbiotic blend of Czechs, Germans, Jews, and a range of other nationalities. Like the Czechs, the Germans too were proud of their history and heritage. Hugo Iltis (1882–1952), a Jew who considered himself a German, was thought to have stated the following at the first meeting of the *Deutsche Gesellschaft für Wissenschaft und Kunst* (German Society for Science and Art): "Today we are alone, separated from the great German nation, and we must unite to preserve our German culture, knowledge, and art." The year was 1919 and Brno was reveling in its new-found Czech identity and rejoicing in the glory of the newly established Czechoslovak Republic.

How painful the rude awakening into Hitler's rising ideology must have been. How painful the realization that German scientists were now distorting genetics in the service of the perverted teachings of eugenics. Iltis himself must have suffered greatly, especially as he was a highly educated and erudite man. He had studied biology and botany at the University of Zurich in Switzerland under Arnold Dodel-Port, a disciple of the famous Munich scientist Carl von Nageli, who was himself involved in a lively correspondence with Mendel, whom he called a friend. He received his PhD in Botany in 1905 at the University of Prague.

Hugo Iltis dedicated his life to safeguarding and defending Mendel's work. He discovered, collected, and used many of Mendel's original writings in his 1924 biography *Gregor Johann Mendel, Leben, Werk, und Wirking* (*Gregor Johann Mendel: Life, Work, and Impact*, Berlin: Springer, 1924; English trans. 1932), the best source on Mendel, even today. He interviewed many of Mendel's relatives, colleagues, pupils, and acquaintances. He raised the funds for the Mendel Memorial in 1910 and gave the commemorative speech at its unveiling. A dedicated educator, he founded and directed Brno's *Masaryk Volkshochschule* (Masaryk People's University, named after the first president of the independent Czechoslovakia) from 1921–1938. And he founded and curated the Mendel Museum in Brno from 1932 to 1937, in which he deposited many of Mendel's writings and relics. He assuredly understood not only Mendel's great scientific contribution to the science of genetics, but also its very human aspect. He saw it as the work of a Christian with great respect for the principle of providing help to one another. In this case, help for farmers, growers, and breeders.

Hugo Iltis honored his German nature yet always showed respect for human nature. He fought against pseudoscientific theories designed to belittle others and destroy, erase, and discredit diversity. He dismantled Nazi eugenics in his *Der Mythus von Blut und Rasse* (*The Myth of Blood and Race*, 1936), the translation of which is included in this book. He likely realized how brutal and cruel the regime gaining power west of Czechoslovakia's borders was proving to be, yet still professed a positive view of humankind. As a result, he and his family were soon forced to flee their homeland in fear for their lives. Nevertheless he left behind a memento – and a legacy.

Today is once again a time to demonstrate our respect for the truth and our inner humanity, values promoted by Hugo Iltis throughout his work. Like many native sons and daughters, he must be remembered in his home town of Brno and throughout the world. However, the very fact that you are now about to begin reading a book penned by a scientist on the eve of the rise of Nazi terror is a sign that examining the past in search of answers to present questions is indeed a worthwhile enterprise. Hugo Iltis deserves our utmost respect. Not only for his scientific work, but also for his courage and dedication to the truth, although doing so threatened his very existence.

Ondřej Dostál
Director, Mendel Museum of Masaryk university
Brno, Czech Republic

INTRODUCTION

HUGO ILTIS: PIONEER OF RESISTANCE TO SCIENTIFIC RACISM

1. Biographical Overview

Hugo Iltis was a brilliant science educator, a highly accomplished botanist, and the pioneering biographer of Gregor Mendel, the founder of modern genetics. Iltis saw that the new science of genetics had not only fundamental scientific significance, but also revolutionary social implications. He was prescient in understanding the potential danger of the misapplication of hereditary biology in furthering racial prejudice and mass destruction of those identified as racially inferior. Iltis forthrightly stated that inferior races did not exist, and that the idea of a superior Aryan race was wholly false. He saw how race theory posed colossal threats to those social groups deemed by Nazi scientists to be racial undesirables. He spent the decade before the Nazi takeover of Czechoslovakia in 1938 campaigning against what he called "*Rassismus,*" meaning racism. Indeed, Iltis claimed to have invented the term *Rassismus* – so as to expose how "racism was a malicious and dangerous weapon for political struggle" in the hands of the Nazis.[1]

Iltis kept marvellously detailed diaries with his notes, letters, and documents, which convey details of his passionate campaign against Nazi racism. Key texts arising from Iltis's dedicated agitation against race theory are presented here. He devoted "all his strength to fight Nazism and race theory" over the decade

---

1   Hugo Iltis (under pseudonym Dr. Wolf Bodansky), "Racism: Intellectual Poison Gas," in *Race in Science and Politics* (*Rasse in Wissenschaft und Politik*, Prague: Wahrheit, 1935), trans. Kareem James Abu-Zeid, see this volume, paragraph one. On Hugo Iltis, see Paul Weindling, "Hugo Iltis," in *Blood and Homeland: Eugenics and Racial Nationalism in Central and Southeast Europe, 1900–1940*, ed. Marius Turda and Paul J. Weindling (Budapest: Central European University Press, 2007), pp. 270–280.

1928–38, until finally having to escape Czechoslovakia for the United States.[2] He was such a forthright critic that when the Nazis entered Brünn they headed straight to where Iltis had lived in order to shoot him, as they had marked him down as a dangerous opponent.[3]

Hugo Iltis was born on 11 April 1882 in Brünn (in Czechoslovakian, Brno), then in multi-ethnic Austria-Hungary, from 1919 in the new state of Czechoslovakia, and today in the Czech Republic. Brünn was the second-largest city of the new republic with some 50,000 Germans, and some 12,000 German- and Czech-speaking Jews, only several hundred of whom survived the Holocaust. Importantly, Brünn was where Gregor Mendel (1822–1884), the pioneer of genetics, discovered the laws of heredity. Iltis studied botany at the Universities of Zurich and at the University of Prague (Charles University), where he received his PhD in 1905. In 1905 Iltis became a teacher at the German High School (*Deutsches Gymnasium*). He was a renowned leader of botanical field trips. Brünn/Brno was a linguistically mixed, culturally vibrant, and economically dynamic location, situated between Prague and Vienna, and not too far from central German locations such as Jena, which was the cradle of German Darwinism. The Nazis made Brünn the capital of Moravia, and it was visited by Hitler soon after the German occupation.

Iltis served the wounded as head of an Austrian field hospital during WW I. Stationed in the Italian Dolomites, he was waist-deep in water for long periods, resulting in chronic rheumatism. In 1919 a new era opened with the founding of the Czechoslovak Republic and its first elected President Tomáš Masaryk (1850–1937). There were distressing incidents, such as when the Mendel monument (produced with funds raised by Iltis and inaugurated in 1910 to the music of the Germanic Richard Wagner and the Czech Bedřich Smetana) was defaced. But liberal and socialist Germans, although a minority, found the new republic progressive, and supportive of German cultural institutions. Iltis was appointed Privatdozent (university lecturer) in botany and genetics in 1911 at the German Polytechnic (Deutsche Technische-Hochschule/German Technical University) in Brünn. In 1921, after Tomáš Masaryk's presidential

---

2   American Philosophical Society (hereafter APS), Iltis to L.C. Dunn, June 2, 1947.

3   Hugh Iltis personal information.

inauguration, he founded and directed the Masaryk *Volkshochschule* (Masaryk People's University), which became a thriving institution for adult education.

Iltis married Anni Liebscher (a distant relative of Mendel) in 1922. Anni was tireless in devotedly supporting her husband. Their first son (referred to by a correspondent as "F1") Fred (Wilfried Gregor) was born on 20 April 1923, and their second son Hugh (Hellmut[4]) was born on 7 April 1925. Both were in the US army in World War II. Fred served in the Southern Pacific, and then developed research in entomology and parasitology, teaching biology at California State University, San Jose. Hugh served first in artillery and then in Military Intelligence, discovering among Himmler's captured papers in Heidelberg details of the murderous experiments at the Dachau concentration camp.[5] Hugh published on the devastation wreaked by the Nazis on Brno and especially on sites associated with Mendel.[6] Hugh became a distinguished botanist, from 1957 at the University of Wisconsin, Madison.

2. Biographer of Mendel

In 1906 Hugo Iltis was elected Secretary for the *Naturforschender Verein* (Natural History Society) in Brünn. Gregor Mendel had published momentous but at the time largely overlooked papers on plant hybridization in the Society's *Transactions*.[7] In 1910, Iltis raised funds for the Mendel Memorial in Brno (see above), and was Secretary for the International Committee for the Mendel Memorial. Geneticists from throughout the world contributed.[8] He was

---

4   The name was a tribute to a socialist admired by Hugo Iltis.

5   Paul Weindling, *Nazi Medicine and the Nuremberg Trials: From Medical War Crimes to Informed Consent* (Basingstoke: Palgrave Macmillan, 2004), p. 76. Author's notes on recollections of Hugh Iltis, 9–13 March 2008.

6   Hugh H. Iltis, A Visit to Gregor Mendel's Home, *Journal of Heredity*, vol. 38 (1947), 162–66.

7   *Verhandlungen des naturforschenden Vereines Brünn*, 1856 to 1863.

8   A. G. Cock, "Bateson's Impressions at the Unveiling of the Mendel Monument at Brno in 1910," *Folia Mendeliana*, vol. 17 (1982), pp. 217–223.

also the Secretary for the Mendel Centenary in 1922, a celebration of the 100th anniversary of Mendel's birth.

Iltis took a pioneering interest in the biography of Gregor Mendel. In 1922 he organized an exhibition of personal items owned by Mendel on the occasion of the centennial celebrations of his birth. His celebratory speech stated that although Mendel was German, he was an enemy of grotesque forms of nationalism. Mendel was a product of racial crossing, analogous to the study made by Eugen Fischer (1874–1967, Professor of anthropology and eugenics at the Kaiser Wilhelm Institute of Anthropology and later a member of the Nazi party) of the Rehoboth Bastards.[9] Iltis was already challenging racial prejudice, while building national identity, and international contacts. Iltis consulted documents, artefacts, and interviews for his Mendel biography. Published in German in 1924 under the title *Gregor Johann Mendel: Leben, Werk und Wirkung* (*Gregor Johann Mendel: Life, Work, and Impact* [Berlin: J. Springer, 1924]), it was a pioneering and landmark study.[10]

Iltis projected the historical image of Mendel as a progressive-minded German scientist whose discoveries would be used for the social improvement of mankind. For all its scholarly merits, this secular and scientifically oriented account antagonized Catholics and German nationalists. Translated as the "Life of Mendel," its publication in English in 1932 earned Iltis further international recognition. Iltis was a dedicated lecturer. He supported the Central Office for Education of the German Socialist Workers Party in the Czechoslovak Republic (*Zentralstelle für das Bildungswesen in der Deutschen sozialdemokratischen Arbeiterpartei in der Tschechoslowakischen Republik*, illustrated below).

---

9 *Pamětní spis ku oslavě stých narozenin J. G. Mendela* (Prague: nákladem Fr. Borového, 1925). *Eugenická knihovna*, 3, 12–13. Eugen Fischer, *Die Rehobother Bastards und das Bastardierungsproblem beim Menschen* (*The Rehoboth Bastards and the Problem of Miscegenation among Humans*) (Jena, 1913).

10 Hugo Iltis, *Gregor Johann Mendel: Leben, Werk und Wirkung*. Herausgegeben mit Unterstützung des Ministeriums für Schulwesen und Volkskultur in Prag. Julius Springer, 1924. English edition published London: Allen & Unwin, 1932.

Zentralstelle für das Bildungswesen der Deutschen sozialdemokratischen Arbeiterpartei in der Tschechoslowakischen Republik

His commitment to lecturing on science for public enlightenment and social improvement meant criss-crossing the country to deliver lectures on topics such as "Theories of Heredity and Human Betterment (*Menschheitsaufstieg*), and the Struggle for Darwinism."[11] One journey alone in March 1922 involved a 3 AM start, and twelve hours of rail travel to deliver a lecture in the northern spa town of Bilin (Bilina).

Iltis continued to publish on science and socialism: A tract on this subject, *Naturwissenschaft und Sozialismus* (*Science and Socialism*), appeared in 1926.[12] He was a gifted publicist. He founded and edited the science education journal *Licht ins Volk* (*Light to the People*). He wrote many pamphlets and frequently gave radio broadcasts to disseminate his creed of socialist eugenics. Iltis used the term "Eugenetik" and avoided racial terminology when speaking to groups of socialist ethnic Germans on the peripheries of the new Czechoslovakia.

Iltis's network stretched to Red Vienna of the 1920s, where the socialist municipalty pioneered mass housing as part of ambitious social welfare schemes. He cultivated contacts with socialists, notably the leading Austrian-Czech Marxist and critic of Soviet Bolshevism, Karl Kautsky (1854–1938), to whom Iltis sent a copy of his Mendel biography on 18 May 1929, and the left-wing embryologist and Darwinist, Julius Schaxel (1887–1943). A German Worker Radio broadcast by Iltis in July 1930 was on the topic of "*Planwirtschaft mit Menschen*"—the planned human economy.

---

11 Hugo Iltis, *Diary*, 21 March 1921, Hugo Iltis Papers, University of Wisconsin, Madison.

12 Hugo Iltis, *Naturwissenschaft und Sozialismus*, 1926.

3. Kammerer: Martyr for a Socialist Biology

Iltis cultivated links to zoologists in Vienna, particularly to the socialist Lamarckian zoologist Paul Kammerer (1880–1926) at the Vivarium— a zoological institute founded by Hans Leo Przibram in 1902. The Vivarium was celebrated as an institute for biological experimentation, where animals were studied over generations under differing environmental conditions. Iltis and Kammerer began correspondence in 1910, and Iltis invited Kammerer to lecture in Brünn in 1912.[13] Pre-1914 Vienna saw a stimulating mix of ideas on biologically based social evolution: the idea of a human economy was advocated by Austrian socialist Rudolf Goldscheid (1870–1931), and by the charismatic social democrat Julius Tandler (1869–1936), who developed the idea of constitutional anatomy.[14] When Iltis was on the high alpine Italian front during the First World War, he remained in touch with Kammerer.

Kammerer's central interest was species change. He set out to show the direct effects of environmental factors. The midwife toad was taken as key evidence, but in 1926 the evidence was exposed as faked, and Kammerer committed suicide. The suicide of his friend and colleague shocked Iltis, who closely examined the tragic circumstances. Iltis drew the conclusion that the injecting of black ink into the specimen was a right-wing plot to discredit Kammerer, the falsification being carried out by a treacherous lab assistant. Iltis gathered materials for a full-scale biography of Kammerer, drawing on information provided by Przibram and others at the Vivarium, in order to rehabilitate Kammerer's reputation.[15] The onset of the threat of racist biology diverted Iltis. The Vivarium legacy was tragic. Only in December 1939 (two months after the outbreak of war) did Przibram move to Amsterdam,

---

13 Paul Kammerer, *"Mendelsche Regeln und Vererbung erworbener Eigenschaften,"* *Verhandlungen des naturforschenden Vereines in Brünn* 49 (1911): 72–110.

14 Paul Weindling, "A City Regenerated: Eugenics, Race and Welfare in Interwar Vienna," Deborah Holmes and Lisa Silverman (ed.), *Interwar Vienna: Culture between Tradition and Modernity* (New York: Camden House, 2009), 81–113.

15 Klaus Taschwer, *Der Fall Kammerer* (Munich: Carl Hanser, 2016), 24, 107, 144.

but tragically died in 1944 in the Theresienstadt concentration camp. Most other zoologists underwent the forced emigration procedures instituted by Eichmann, whereby they were only allowed to emigrate after being fleeced of their belongings.

4. Against Racism

During the 1920s Iltis saw the rising dangers of the anti-socialist and anti-semitic right, which was gaining in influence, and criticized anti-semitism among certain Czech socialists. The extent of his preoccupation with social questions is evident from his copious diary entries. Iltis had first-hand acquaintance with the scientists whom he came to recognize as dangerous progenitors of racial theory. He corresponded with the leading German eugenicist, Fritz Lenz (1887–1976, described by Iltis as "the precise geneticist and racist"), who he considered to be a geneticist of some sophistication. Along with the plant geneticist Erwin Baur and anthropologist Eugen Fischer (1874–1967), Lenz published a leading handbook of human heredity in 1921.[16] In 1930 Lenz came out in support of National Socialism as the best way to realize eugenic measures. Iltis saw the dangerous direction of a colleague who was soon to advise the SS (Hitler's paramilitary "*Schutzstaffel*") on hereditary procedures.

Iltis participated in the International Congress of Genetics in Berlin in 1927. The Congress accompanied the inauguration of the Kaiser Wilhelm Institute for Anthropology, with Eugen Fischer as its Director. Iltis thus observed first-hand German geneticists who became leading figures under National Socialism. In 1928 Iltis published on eugenics in the left book review *Bücherwarte* in Berlin. At this stage he dismissed the theorist of Aryan superiority Joseph Arthur Comte de Gobineau (1816–1882) and the racialist writer Houston Stewart Chamberlain (1855–1927), as well as the Nordic racial ideologists Hans Günther (1891–1968)

---

16 Fritz Lenz, *Menschliche Auslese und Rassenhygiene* (Munich: J. F. Lehmanns Verlag, 1921). H. Fange-rau, "*Der 'Baur-Fischer-Lenz' in der Buchkritik 1921-1940: Eine quantifizierende Untersuchung zur zeit-genössischen Rezeption rassenhygienischer Theorien*," *Medizinhistorisches Journal* 38, 2003 (1): 57–81.

and Fritz Lenz, as racists. He was prepared to seriously engage with and partly accept the work of Eugen Fischer, although he remained critical of his linking psychological to physical types. He accepted certain "objective" eugenic measures as marriage certificates, and endorsed the social hygiene of Alfred Grotjahn (1869–1931), which focused on the "hygiene of reproduction."

In spring 1931 Iltis taught at the *Volkshochschule* on the "Race Question," covering the topics: what is race; race in original forms; race and degeneration; and race and politics. During this time he published on the "Race Research and the Race Question" (*Rassenforschung und Rassenfrage*) in *Der Kampf. Sozialistische Monatshefte* (*The Struggle. International Review of Socialism*). He broadcast on the radio against Nordic race theory. He lectured in the free city of Danzig on "Racial Research and the Race Question" as part of a series of lectures on Science and Socialism.[17] And on 2 November 1933 he lectured in Bratislava about "Race, Racial Arrogance, and Hate."[18]

Hitler's coming to power in Germany in 1933 increased pressure on Czechoslovakia. There was polarization between the ethnic "Sudeten Germans," who supported Nazism, and liberal and socialist Germans, who supported the Czechoslovak Republic. There were rising numbers of anti-Nazi German refugees in Czechoslovakia, and Iltis provided hospitality for refugees. In May 1934 the Second International Conference of Socialist Doctors in the Czechoslovak Republic was held in Brünn. The city was located close to Austrofascist Austria. The programme—documented by Iltis in his diary—included Theodor Gruschka (1888–1967) from Aussig (a town on the Northern frontier) speaking on the first year of Nazi public health, as well as noted international participants, addressing the issue of "Racial Hygiene and Socialism."[19]

---

17 Iltis, *Diary 1930-1931*, clipping for the Danzig lecture series.

18 Iltis, *Diary 1933*, "*Rasse, Rassenhochmut, Rassenhass.*"

19 *Internationales ärztliches Bulletin*, Prague, vol. 4 (1937), Issue 4–5 (May-June), pp. 45–56: "*Eugenik und Rassismus.*" Eckard Hansen, Michael Heisig, Stephan Leibfried [et al.]: *Seit über einem Jahrhundert...: verschüttete Alternativen in der Sozialpolitik* (Cologne, 1981). Paul Weindling, "Shattered Alternatives in Medicine," *History Workshop Journal*, no. 16 (1983), 152–157.

Iltis continued writing and speaking against racism. He gave radio lectures on race, for example *"Die Rassen der Menschheit"* in December 1935. He distinguished between "racist ideology" and science. His forthright radio talk in 1936 stated that there was no such entity as a German race or German blood, and that the idea of a Nordic race was wholly bogus.[20] In 1936 he published the essay *"Was ist Rasse?"* in the Masaryk College journal *Licht ins Volk* for public enlightenment. In 1937 he lectured in Prague on "Racism and Scientific Change."[21] His new term "Rassismus" corresponded with similarly new French terms "racisme" and "raciste." A new anti-racist vocabulary was forged on an international front to combat Aryan and Nordic race theories as wholly unscientific but politically menacing.

5. Books Denouncing Racism

In the 1930s, Hugo Iltis published the three important booklets, translated in this volume, that denounced Nazi racist arguments—all rooted in his study of Mendelian genetics and exposing the flaws in eugenics. His work was published by the socialist Urania organization in Jena. In 1930 his *Volkstümliche Rassenkunde* (Popular Race Theory) was serialized and first appeared as a set of political brochures, ensuring wide circulation, before being published as a book—relevant portions of which are translated here. This was designed to strike at the heart of the groundswell of support for Nazism in Thuringia, and was targeted at the Nordic racial theorist Günther (see above), who was appointed to a chair of racial theory at Jena University in 1930. Iltis denounced Günther as a "race messiah" who based his Nordic theories on spurious statistics. Iltis joined other critics— the Austrian social scientist Friedrich Hertz (1878–1964); the radiologist from the spa town of Karlsbad, Ignaz Zollschan (1877–1944); and the French historian

---

20 Hugo Iltis, *"Das Rassenproblem in Europa," Das Radiojournal*, 15 January 1936. Note by Fred Il-tis, "Papa's Radio Lectures, Many deal with Racism. German Radio Hour on Radio Brno." Cf Thomas Etzemüller, *Auf der Suche nach dem Nordischen Menschen. Die deutsche Rassenanthropolo-gie in der modernen Welt* (Bielefeld: transcript, 2015).

21 Hugo Iltis, *"Der Rassismus im Wandel der Wissenschaft," Prager Zeitschrift* (1 April 1937).

of German civilization, Edmond Vermeil (1878–1964)—in attacking Günther as unscientific and politically dangerous.[22] Iltis foresaw the ominous possibilities of extermination policies, realizing that anthropologists were guilty of supporting genocide under colonialism. He rejected the notion of the degenerative effects of racial interbreeding as a political falsehood.

Iltis's second major attack appeared in 1935 in his edited book *Rasse in Wissenschaft und Politik* (Race in Science and Politics). This volume began with an opening essay by Iltis and a closing article written by him under the pseudonym Dr. Wolf Bodansky (both translated here). The intervening articles were all written by Czechoslovak and German anti-racial experts. The second essay was by Frantisek Weyr (1879–1951), a professor of law at the Masaryk University, who was arrested by Gestapo in 1943. The third was by Jan Bělehrádek (1896–1980), a biologist trained in Brünn, who became a professor at Charles University in Prague. During the war he was hidden but finally imprisoned in Theresienstadt, where he survived but was to clash with communists and forced into exile. The fourth essay was by Vojtěch Suk (1789–1967), or in his original German name Adalbert Sük, an anthropologist of a younger generation who became the head of the new Anthropological Institute at the Masaryk University in Brno. Alfred Fuchs (1892–1941), who wrote the fifth essay, was a leading intellectual of Jewish origin who converted to Catholicism. He was head of the intelligence unit of the Czechoslovak Ministry of Foreign Affairs under Edvard Beneš (1884–1948) and remained after Beneš's election to President in 1935. He declined to emigrate in 1939 and stayed in Prague. He was imprisoned by the Prague Gestapo and sent to the Dachau concentration camp, where he was tortured and died. The sixth essay was by Hans Reiner (1896–1991), an existentialist German philosopher who published on the topic of science and objectivity.[23]

---

22 Vermeil Edmond, *Pangermanisme et racisme. Coup d'oeil d'ensemble sur le racisme allemand avant la guerre mondiale. H.F.K. Günther et la théorie du Nordisme* (Paris: Races et Racisme, 1937). Amos Morris-Reich, "Race, Ideas, and Ideals: A Comparison of Franz Boas and Hans F. K. Günther," *History of European Ideas,* vol. 32 (3), 2006, pp. 313–332.

23 My thanks to Michal V. Šimůnek for this information. Antonín Kostlán, Michal V. Šimůnek eds, *Disappeared Science. Biographical Dictionary of Jewish Scholars from Bohemia and Moravia - Vic-*

The third booklet translated here is Iltis's *Der Mythus von Blut und Rasse* (The Myth of Blood and Race), published in Vienna in 1936. In the introductory chapter, Iltis attacked the "poison gas" ideas of Nazi racial purity. He appealed directly to Viennese public opinion, calling for popular mobilization against racism. At the same time he targeted academic anthropologists as a core Nazi group, not least because Nazi German anthropologists believed that the Czechs could be Germanized. On the one hand, he appealed to Viennese public opinion to reject racism, and on the other for a world court of science to condemn racism as a product of power politics, hate, phantasy, and lies.[24] He targeted the academic anthropologists as a key Nazi group.

Iltis sent the book on 9 June 1936 to the Columbia University anthropologist Franz Boas (1858–1942), who, like Iltis, saw "*Rassismus*" as a "*Scheinwissenschaft*" (pseudoscience), suggesting that it might be translated. Boas, responding on 23 June, said that he was glad that Iltis was opposed to "the present curse of race," and he would see whether an American publisher might be interested.[25]

6. The International Coalition Against Race Theory Takes Shape

Iltis's critique of Nazi race theory as unscientific grew out of his commitment to Mendelism. Out of his 1935 edited book, *Race in Science and Politics*, an anti-racist scientific coalition formed. In so doing, Iltis had to put aside some reservations regarding Jewish anthropologist Ignaz Zollschan (1877–1934), who had strong commitments to preserving Jewish cultural identity. Zollschan's writings were Lamarckian in contrast to Iltis's Mendelism, and were concerned to demonstrate that Jews did not constitute a race in a biological sense but rather

---

tims of Nazism, 1939-1945 (Prague: Institute of Contemporary History of the Academy of Sciences of the Czech Republic, 2013). Soňa Štrbáňová, Antonín Kostlán eds., *Sto českých vědců v exilu* (Prague: Academia, 2011).

24 See review in *Internationales ärztliches Bulletin*, vol. 3 (1936), 136.

25 American Philosophical Society (APS), Boas Papers, Correspondence, Iltis to Boas 6, June 1938; Boas to Iltis.

in a cultural sense. Iltis believed, along with others, that ideas of a Jewish race and of an Aryan race were both false. Whereas Iltis was gifted in critical analysis of racist science in lectures and publications, Zollschan was primarily an organizer of an anti-racist coalition. To resist the unscientific basis of racial science, Zollschan established national committees at the Academy of Sciences in Prague and Vienna, as well as in London, under the auspices of the Royal Anthropological Society and Royal Society, and through the eminent anthropologist Franz Boas (1858–1942) at Columbia University in the United States. He hoped that an international panel would conduct an inquiry into race and evaluate racial theories. Iltis approached the politically exiled Vienna anatomist Julius Tandler (1869–1936), a distant relative, to propose a critique of the racial concept. Tandler had been dismissed in 1934 for his socialism. In response to Iltis, Tandler (along with his student, Jewish anatomist Harry Sicher, 1889–1974, who fled Austria to Chicago in 1939) prioritized a critical analysis of the key concepts. Tandler had already raised the possibility of finding Russian collaborators—but here there was no response.[26]

Appealing directly to Viennese public opinion, Iltis called for popular mobilization against racism as a dangerous disease. The public needed to be immunized against its spread. He targeted academic anthropologists as a core Nazi group, not least because German anthropologists believed that the Czechs could be Germanized.

Iltis represented the Czechoslovakian League against Anti-Semitism at an international congress held in Paris in 1937. Zollschan gained the support of Czech political leaders, particularly the philosophically-inclined Czechoslovak president Tomáš Masaryk; while the foreign minister, later president, Edvard Beneš lobbied the supine League of Nations. Support grew for the *Ligue Internationale Contre l'Antisémitisme* (International League Against Racism and Anti-Semitism, LICA), which included Masaryk, Beneš, and Albert Einstein as members of its Committee of Honor.

Iltis and Zollschan worked towards a common end both nationally and internationally. Both hoped that the anti-eugenic Catholic Church could

---

26 APS Tandler to Iltis, 8 Oct 1935.

become an ally against Nazi racism. Some German Catholic theologians were in favor of eugenics, such as Hermann Muckermann (1877–1962), the co-founder of the Kaiser Wilhelm Institute for Anthropology in Berlin, described by Iltis as "the circumspect, genteel Jesuit and racist." The condemnation of eugenics in the Papal encyclical *Casti Conubii* (On Christian Marriage) in 1930 gave rise to the hope, largely unrealistic, as it turned out, that the Church would take a firm stand against Nazi race ideology and policies. Zollschan approached Cardinal Theodor Innitzer (1875–1955), the Archbishop of Vienna, and Iltis approvingly cited Cardinal Faulhaber's writings against Aryan race theory. At the very least they hoped to expose the activities of anti-Semitic priests, such as Pater (Wilhelm) Schmidt (1868–1954) in Vienna. In pursuing this goal Zollschan had two private audiences with Pope Pius XI in 1934 and 1935. A Papal Encyclical condemning race theory *De Humani Generis* (on false opinions threatening to undermine the foundations of Catholic doctrine) was prepared but never promulgated.[27]

In contrast to Iltis, Hertz and Zollschan were more sympathetic to Lamarckism than to Mendelian population genetics. By way of contrast, Julian Huxley (1887–1975), who represented the public face of British biology in the 1930s, disapproved on scientific grounds of Zollschan's citation of the environmentalist "engramme theory" advocated by the German biologist Richard W. Semon (1859–1918). By the late 1930s Hertz, Iltis, and Zollschan condemned Nazi racism while simultaneously retaining ideas about population and inheritance.

Zollschan hoped that leading anthropologists would unite under the auspices of the League of Nations to condemn Nazi racism as unscientific. In 1933 Zollschan gained the support of Masaryk, and, in 1936, worked alongside Czech President Beneš at the League of Nations in Geneva, organizing a petition signed by Freud and Masaryk among many others. The large number of German and Austrian intellectuals in Prague during the 1930s (including Hertz, who came to Prague in 1938) resulted in a strident opposition to race theory. Heinrich Mann, Arthur Holitischer, Lion Feuchtwanger, Max Brod, and Heinrich Coudenhove-Kalergi

---

27 Georges Passelecq, Bernard Suchecky, *The Hidden Encyclical of Pius XI* (NY: Harcourt Brace, 1997).

published the pamphlet *Gegen die Phrase vom jüdischen Schädling* (Against the Phrase, Jewish Parasite). Zollschan organized expert groups of anthropologists at the Royal Society of London and the Royal Anthropological Institute of Great Britain and Ireland in 1934; the initiative was strategically important because of an international Anthropological and Ethnological Conference held in London in July to August 1934 and at the Société d'Anthropologie de Paris (Society of Anthropology of Paris) in 1937. By joining forces with the environmentalist anthropologist Boas in New York, he reinforced an international coalition of intellectuals, anthropologists, and scientists against the destruction inherent in Nazi race theory.

Committees were established in Prague, in Vienna (under dental anatomist Harry Sicher) in 1937, in Paris with the campaigning group *Races et Racisme* (Races and Racism), and in London at the Royal Anthropological Society. Here the popular book, *We Europeans: A Survey of 'Racial Problems* (1935), was initiated by the historian of medicine Charles Singer and written by the biologist Julian Huxley, the anthropologist A.C. Haddon, and the demographer A.M. Carr-Saunders. Friedrich Hertz in Halle in 1932 and Fritz Merkenschlager in Kiel were among the few in Germany to courageously oppose Hans Günther's racist ideology.[28] By the mid-1930s Czechoslovakia was in the vanguard of opposition to Nazi race theory. In 1936 an anti-Nazi Society for the Scientific Study of Human Races was founded in Prague. Hertz came in 1938 from Germany to Prague, where there was already a community of anti-Nazi intellectuals, in part due to Iltis's tireless campaigning.

Iltis's calls for a popular mobilization against racism were loud and clear. The International Federation of Eugenics Organizations planned to meet in 1938 at the Baltic resort of Parnu in Estonia, when the issue arose of resisting Nazi eugenics. Against this the German biological anthropologists Eugen Fischer and Otmar Freiherr von Verschuer (1896–1969) enjoyed the backing of Nazi propaganda machinery, and exercised rising influence among other rightward

---

28 Tony Kushner, *We Europeans? Mass-Observation, 'Race' and British Identity in the Twentieth Century* (Aldershot: Ashgate, 2004). Elazir Barkan, *The Retreat of Scientific Racism. Changing Concepts of Race in Britain between the World Wars* (Cambridge: Cambridge University Press, 1992).

leaning Central European eugenicists. Iltis rightly denounced Fischer as "the leader of the racists."

7. Flight to America

With the German annexation of Czechoslovakia's Sudetenland in 1938, Iltis was in mortal peril. He mobilized contacts abroad, notably the musicologist Arnold Walter (1902–1973) in Canada, who detailed the topics on which Iltis could give lectures in the U.S. Albert Einstein also responded on 23 April 1938 with a letter to Franz Boas stating that Professor Iltis's "life is no longer safe in Czechoslovakia" and that "it is our duty to do everything in our power to save this man, while there is still time" (Einstein to Boas, 23 April 1938, reprinted in this volume). Iltis fled to the UK in December 1938 as a place of safety with support from Michael Pease (1890–1966), an agriculturalist at the Genetical Institute of Cambridge and a British Mendelian. As a result of these combined efforts, an American visa and placement for Iltis came through. Through the efforts of Peter Ray Ogden, Iltis was offered a position at the International School in Fredericksburg, Virginia, before moving to Mary Washington College, also in Fredericksburg.

The emigration of Iltis to the United States in 1939 meant that he was able to develop contacts with liberal-minded geneticists, notably Leslie Clarence (L.C.) Dunn (1893–1974). A strident critic of the Ku Klux Klan, Iltis found that once again he faced racism on his doorstep. His characteristic response was to plan the founding of an Institute for the Study of the Problems of the Human Races. Czechoslovak political support for his endeavors can be seen in a letter from Iltis to Czech President Beneš on May 17, 1943.

The culmination of the anti-racist efforts came in May 1945 with a UNESCO Conference of Allied Ministers of Education, who formed an international Science Commission. This attacked the fallacies of Nazi racial theories as false science and false religion. At the time of the Nuremberg Trials, Iltis wrote a memorandum to three key persons and agencies: Col H.H. Wade of the United Nations War Crimes Commission; the War Crimes Branch Wiesbaden APO

633 U.S. Army; and Justice Jackson's Office, Office of the U.S. Chief of Counsel Nuremberg. Iltis stated that "'Scientific' representatives of German race theory should be prosecuted as war criminals."[29] Col Wade recognized that Iltis was an expert as "he wrote several books and papers opposing and fighting the German race theory." Iltis wrote on 14 October 1945 to Boguslav Ecer, who was the Czech delegate to the International Military Tribunal on "The War Crime of Racism." He sent a list of three groups "who fabricated the mental poison gas of racism." Firstly came "a small group of scientists of good standing and even of fame": Eugen Fischer, Fritz Lenz, Philalet[h]es Kuhn[30], Herman[n] Siemens, W[alter] Scheidt, Agnes Bluhm[31], Ernst Rüdin, O[tto] Reche, [Otto] Aichel[32], Theodor Mollison, Prof. Dr. Much (Vienna)[33], Verschuer, and Ernst Lehmann. The second was "a group of popular writers wrapped in the cover of science and also in the poison to the so-called intelligence": the names which he cited were Hans Günther, [Robert] Mielke (Berlin)[34], B.K. Schultz[35], Fritz Kern[36],

---

29 United Nations Archives UNWCC File C-1, Iltis to Boguslav Ecer. Also Iltis to Ecer, 14 January 1946. United Nations War Crimes Commission. Research Branch, Bulletin 18, 26 November 1945. Michal V. Šimůnek, "Informed Testimonies. Physicians' Accounts of Nazi Medical Experiments in the Context of Early Czechoslovak War Crimes Investigations, 1945–1948," *From Clinic to Concentration Camp: Reassessing Nazi Medical and Racial Research, 1933–1945* (Abingdon: Routledge, 2017).

30 Philalethes Kuhn, born in 1870, was an expert in tropical medicine and racial hygiene; he had died in 1937.

31 Agnes Bluhm, born in 1862, was a pioneer of racial hygiene; she had died in 1943.

32 Otto Aichel, born in 1871, was an anatomist and anthropologist linked to Rudolf Hess, the deputy Führer; he had died in 1935.

33 Rudolf Much was an anthropologist, Nazi activist, and anti-Semite; he had died in 1936.

34 Robert Mielke, born in 1863, was an ethnologist; he had died in 1935.

35 Bruno Kurt Schultz was a leading SS anthropologist, and head of the RuSHA (*Rasse- und Siedlungshauptamt-SS*; The Main SS Race and Settlement Office)..

36 Fritz Kern, author of *Nationale Erbgesundheitslehre und Volksaufartung : Richtlinien f. d. Unterricht.*

Ludwig Clauss, [Martin] Staemmler, and J[akob] Graf[37]. Third, "a great number of cheaper or finer politicians who used racism to stir up the people such as Goebbels, Rosenberg, Streicher, etc."[38]

There was some interest in having a Second Medical Trial at Nuremberg against Nazi race scientists—notably Otmar von Verschuer (1896–1969), supporter of the Auschwitz scientist Josef Mengele (1911–1979), who selected which victims would be sent to the gas chambers and who retained several hundred Jewish twins for genetic research.[39] The proposed second trial would have been constructed on the basis of Iltis's important evidence. However, sterilization by means of X-rays at Auschwitz (the case against SS officer Rudolf Brandt, 1909–1948), euthanasia, a euphemism for mass murder (the case against physician Karl Brandt, 1904–1948), and eugenics, creation of an elite within the SS (the case against Hellmut Poppendick/Poppendieck, 1902–1994, a protégé of Lenz), were all successfully prosecuted at the Nuremberg Trials (unsuccessful was the case against the German-Czech dermatologist from Komotau, Adolf Pokorny, b. 1895, for using an herbal-based method of sterilization).[40] In the longer term the UNESCO Declaration on Race of 1951—"Statement on the Nature of Race and Race Differences"—could be considered a legacy.

Hugo Iltis died on 22 June 1952 in Fredericksburg, Virginia. The appreciation published by L.C. Dunn portrayed the momentous significance of Iltis's achievements as scientist, educator and crusader against deadly racism:

---

37 Jakob Graf, born in 1891, was author of the Nazi school textbook on *Biologie für Oberschule und Gymnasium*.

38 Grateful thanks to Michal V. Šimůnek, who kindly provided transcripts and copies.

39 Paul Weindling, "'Tales from Nuremberg': the Kaiser Wilhelm Institute for Anthropology and Allied Medical War Crimes Policy," Doris Kaufmann (ed.), *Geschichte der Kaiser-Wilhelm-Gesellschaft im Nationalsozialismus. Bestandsaufnahme und Perspektiven der Forschung*, 2 vols., (Göttingen: Wallstein Verlag, 2000), 621–38.

40 Paul Weindling, *Victims and Survivors of Nazi Human Experiments: Science and Suffering in the Holocaust* (London: Bloomsbury, 2014).

"He was known as the declared enemy of the pseudosciences on which Hitler's state was founded. His great energy and intensity of purpose enabled him to carry on simultaneously his activities as scientist, biographer, educator, organizer, and writer for the public. . . . In reviewing the life of a colleague and friend, one sees the essence of the scientific calling itself. . . . of a spirit in which courage, integrity, and devotion . . . are essential ingredients."[41]

Paul Weindling
Oxford Brookes University
Oxford, United Kingdom

---

41   L.C. Dunn, "Hugo Iltis: 1882–1952," *Science* (2 January 1953), No. 3027, 3–4, quotations on 3 and 4.

POPULAR RACE THEORY

Excerpts

By Hugo Iltis

Translated from the German by Christopher W. Reid, PhD

German edition: *Volkstümliche Rassenkunde*

"Urania"-Verlagsgesellschaft M.B.H., Jena, 1930

PREFACE AND INTRODUCTION

About 80 years ago, French Count [Joseph Arthur] Gobineau [1816–1882][1], an original writer of great imagination and little criticism, theorized that in the life of a people and its fate, race was the decisive factor. He also proposed that the noble Aryan race should be viewed as having been responsible for creating the greatest cultures.

While Gobineau's fantastical hypothesis attracted the attention of only a small circle, the new, more sophisticated representation of Gobineau's doctrine was of the utmost, and most ominous, importance in the citation-laden books of the German-writing Englishman, [Houston Stewart] Chamberlain [1855–1927][2], especially for the thinking and the actions of the German ruling class before the war. As science has since proven that the concept "Aryan" can only be applied to languages, that an "Aryan race" does not exist, nor has ever existed, Chamberlain simply replaced "Aryan" with "Germanic." At the same time, he extended the scope of this term enormously by making not only the British and Americans German, but he also claimed the elites of the French, Italians, Russians, etc. for the Teutonic world.

[For these writers] all cultural progress stems from "Germanentum," whose noblest flowering was the piratical Viking culture. Viking-like methods are also applied in *Chamberlain's* scholarship. All the great pioneers of the culture are annexed to the Teutonic world, with Jesus Christ, Michelangelo, among others, being designated Germans without further ado. Wherever this is simply not possible (Spinoza, Confucius, etc.), the achievement is declared inferior, or at least "not creative."

---

1   Joseph Arthur Gobineau, *Essay on the Inequality of the Human Races* (1853–1855); German translation, Ludwig Schemann, *Versuch über die Ungleichheit der Menschenrassen*, 1897).

2   Houston Steward Chamberlain, *The Foundations of the Nineteenth Century*; German edition *Die Grundlagen des 19. Jahrhunderte*, [1899], 14th ed., 1929.

The Chamberlain books found a large audience and had a profound impact, especially in Germany. "The Foundations of the Nineteenth Century" was one of Kaiser Wilhelm II's favorite books. The racial self-aggrandizement, which every educated person should consider as tasteless as an individual's own self-praise, elicited among wide swaths of the German nobility and bourgeoisie the megalomaniacal belief in the "German mission" – that dangerous underestimation of other peoples, which surely may be regarded as one of the underlying causes of [World War I].

One would have thought that the war and its outcome would have spelled the definitive end of racial fanaticism. Blood did not turn out to be "thicker" than water: The Germanic Anglo-Saxons went toe to toe with Germanic Teutons; the French were the military victors, and the international captains of finance the economic winners. Nonetheless, after the war, the belief in race rose like a phoenix from the ashes. What had previously been advocated by more or less gifted dilettantes had now made inroads into a *part* of official scholarship.

The modern proponents of evaluative racial research appropriated the *Gobineau-Chamberlain* hypothesis, which I shall call the "racist conception of history" or simply "racism," and expanded on it. Relying on the findings of genetic research, they assert that the innate race, which has been decisive for major historical movements, could neither be influenced by the environment in general or the relations of production in particular, and that these factors only have secondary importance for the course of history. Racism thus represents a deliberate contrast to Marxism. It establishes the ideology for bourgeois imperialism, as well as for petty-bourgeois nationalism, and provides a legal basis for the stronger – in other words, noble – races to prey on the weaker ones. Moreover, through the determination that ruling qualities of the upper classes, and the inferiority of the lower classes, are innate, it also confirms the inevitability of the class structure of the class state. It thus complements the human-established law of inheritance with one established by nature.

Racism represents the conservative position in relation to revolutionary Marxism. In the years after the war, it gained in significance and acceptance, especially in Germany. Due to the adverse circumstances, the struggle for existence, that is the "struggle to find work," became increasingly bitter and rancorous. Racism, which made the "right to a good job" dependent only on an innate qualification, the "good race," not the position, and offered the opportunity to dispose with all "racially inferior," albeit able competitors, was particularly well received at German universities.

A torrent of racist literature burst forth, and an entire racial mythology arose under the guise of science. Because this onslaught went almost completely unopposed by the socialist side, the bitterness and fanaticism with which it was represented did not need to appear entirely comprehensible to those unfamiliar with its ideological and economic implications. . . .

There is no space in this slim volume for a discussion or a settling of accounts with racism in the narrow sense, specifically with the views of Gobineau, Chamberlain, Günther, among others.[3] This will occur elsewhere. There, it will also be possible to show that while race may not be the "motor of history," it does play a vital role under natural conditions of social development. *Karl Marx*[4] and *Friedrich Engels*[5] neither overlooked nor denied the significance of race. However, as anthropological research was still at an early stage during their lifetime, and a precise distinction was not even made between race and people, they could not consider all the implications of race. It is not the worst effect of racism that it forces us to deal with the race problem, while dialectically promoting our understanding of the significance of race as a natural basis of labor power and, hence, the process of production.

---

3   See also Hugo Iltis, *Rassenwissenschaft und Rassenwahn*, "*Die Gesellschaft*," (Berlin 1927); H. Iltis, *Rassenforschung und Rassenfrage*, "*Sozialistische Bildung*" (Berlin 1929).

4   Karl Marx, *Das Kapital*, vol. I. I, p. 140, 476; Vol. III, p. 325. — *Thesen über Feuerbach*, p. 237ff., 242ff., 245ff. — *Theorien über den Mehrwert*, Vol. III, p. 519. — Cf. also K. A. Wittfogel, *Geopolitik, geographischer Materialismus und Marxismus* (1929), p. 509 ff.

5   Friedrich Engels, cf. Ludwig Woltmann, *Der historische Materialismus* (Düsseldorf: Hermann Michaels, 1900), p. 249.

THE FOUNDATIONS OF RACIAL RESEARCH

When we put a blond northern European beside a woolly hair Sudan Negro and a slant-eyed Chinese, then race appears, at first glance, to be something given, and the racial line is easy to draw. However, if we put certain inhabitants of Russian Asia and eastern Russia between a Chinese and North European, and an Abyssinian and a Sicilian between a Sudan Negro and a North European, then it turns out that racial boundaries are not set by nature, but rather by human beings for the sake of getting an overview, of creating a system. Just as, for example, with the classification of languages into dialects, the number of groups can be increased or reduced, depending on whether one defines them narrowly or more broadly. Especially in a mixed population, as in Europe, the keen observer repeatedly notices new types, which could be described as racial types. Of course, not every physically distinct type is a racial type. Pat and Patachon [a Danish comedy duo of the 1920s-1940s with very different physique], for instance, are certainly very different physically, but these differences have nothing to do with race.

Reflected here is the recurring constitution or bodily types, the study of which is the focus of modern constitution research. Similarly, it would be wrong to speak of a German and a Czech race: Racially, Germans and Czechs, at least in many parts of the Sudetenland, can barely be differentiated, or at most only in regard to different facial expressions shaped by language. They belong to different peoples. It is necessary to sharply distinguish between the two terms, people and race, as well as the respective sciences. As "people," we refer to a group of human beings who are linked by a common culture, and also especially a common language. The science that deals with peoples and their spiritual and material cultural heritage is called ethnography (*Völkerkunde*) or ethnology. Under a "human race," we mean a group of human beings linked by the social acquisition and possession of a sum of hereditary physical characteristics and differentiated from other such groups. Race theory as a part of anthropology (= human science) has the task of studying the human races and describing them according to their existence and development using the scientific method, i.e. objectively and without evaluation.

In our explanation of the term "human race," we deliberately define it only in terms of shared physical characteristics. Of course, there is no doubt that mental and physical features are closely linked. The connections, however, are infinitely complicated: Mental attributes, after all, are not only influenced by race, but, like the body, even more so by environment, tradition, culture and society. They also elude direct observation. But it is precisely because we know nothing or almost nothing for certain today about mental racial characteristics that the door is left wide open for arbitrary assertions. "If there were only physical differences between the races, then the whole issue of race would be irrelevant," concedes [Fritz] Lenz [1887–1976], a well-known racist leader. Nevertheless, this particular significance of race is being kept alive at all costs. This is why knowledge is feigned where only assumptions exist, and it is on the basis of these assumptions that glorifying or disapproving value judgments are made. On the other hand, subjective speculations in a natural science should be held back as much as possible. It is due to the current state of our knowledge, therefore, that we find it useful to comprehend the concept of race in purely physical terms.

Anatomically, the human being is a mammal and part of the natural world. The laws that have been recognized for animals and plants through observation and experiment generally apply to humans as well. If we want to understand the development and existence of the human race, we must familiarize ourselves with the basic biological facts of evolution and heredity. The prevailing doctrine over the centuries was the ancient theological doctrine of immutability and the God-createdness of all living beings, backed by the authority of the Church. Nevertheless, even the idea of a natural evolution was itself the product of a long development, with the names Lamarck, Geoffroy St. Hilaire, Charles Lyell etc., marking its final stages. *Darwin*'s magnum opus *On the Origin of Species* from 1859 was published at an auspicious time and the obstacles to its views no longer stood in the way. The science of the human races also breathed new life into evolutionary thought, as the relationship of the races was reconceived in terms of blood relations. Today, the theory of evolution itself – i.e. the doctrine of natural, ascending development of living things or, as applied to man, the doctrine of the origin of man and the origin of the human races from animal forms – is the common property of scholarship. . . .

   The transformational forces of evolution are confronted by the self-perpetuating forces of heredity. The nature of the organic world can only be understood in terms of the conflict between or the dialectic of propulsive and retentive forces. One who loses sight of how tenaciously organic form strives to preserve itself has just as false an idea as another who sees rigidity in a state of flux. Man – the individual and the human race – is subject to the same laws. Of course, we must keep in mind that, aside from those operative factors in the wider realm of organisms (heredity or congenital tendencies, whose modification is affected by the natural environment, mutation, crossing), human traits, especially mental traits, are also determined by social factors (handed-down or traditional systems, whose modification is affected by the artificial environment, economy, technology, etc.).

* * * *

CLASSIFYING THE HUMAN RACE

The definition and classification of human races is based, on the one hand, on the visible racial characteristics and the geographical distribution of the races, and, on the other, on the findings of pre-historical research or the community of origin. Whereas the first method, i.e. the morphological-geographic method, always runs the risk of only creating artificial groups, combining foreign characteristics, or separating related qualities due to accidental physical similarities or the proximity of races, the genealogical method could make it possible to determine the real pedigree of the human race and thus the natural system, the natural unity, of the human groups. This would be possible, that is, if only the findings of paleontology were not so unclear nor our knowledge of the primitive human races and their relation to the humans living today (unfortunately, this is inherently the case) so sketchy!

Just how far we are still from arriving at a reasonably satisfactory solution is indicated by the fact that almost every researcher represents different views concerning the origin of today's races and their mode of togetherness and relatedness. Indeed, there is not even full agreement on the basic question of whether mankind originated from one animal species (monogenesis) or from several (polygenesis). The most diverse perspectives have been applied for arranging the system of the human races: from Linnaeus, who in his "*Systema Naturae*" from 1758 classified human races according to the four parts of the globe and skin color, to Kant (1775) and Blumenbach (1779), whose five races (white or Caucasian, black or Ethiopian, yellow or Mongolian, brown or Malay, red or Indian) still play a role to this day in textbooks and popular works, and the essays from Virey (1801), Cuvier (1817), Prichard (1830), Huxley (1870), F. Müller and Haeckel (1873), and the more modern systems of Ehrenreich (1897), Sergi (1897), Stratz (1903), Boas (1908); Stratz-Fritsch (1910), Ranke (1912), Wilser (1912), Giuffrida-Ruggeri (1913), Fischer (1922), Haddon (1924), and many others.

Humanity forms a single species, species *homo sapiens*. The fact alone that practically every author delineates the races differently, that almost every feature of a race, however pronounced, appears to be connected by gradations with the respective features of other races, suggests that no sharp boundaries exist. Starting with a similar point of departure, the French anthropologists' school established by [Pierre Paul] Broca [1824–1880] and further built on by [Paul] Topinard [1830–1911], [Joseph] Deniker [1852–1918], among others, contented itself with compiling racial types, without, however, saying anything definitive about their genealogical value. Topinard postulates such racial types in his *"Anthropologie"* 25 [types], as does Deniker in his *"Rassen und Völkerkunde"* 29 [types].

In the racial description that follows, the attempt will be made to identify the most important race types and, taking into account the geographical and paleontological facts, to point out existing relational links. We must remain aware of the fact that the racial picture of mankind today is only a cross-section, only a snapshot, of the human race's ever-changing course of development. Most authors make the mistake of continually trying to depict the evolution of mankind by means of a simple longitudinal section or superficially projecting on to it a family tree. All existing races, even if they originated from a single tribe, have frequently crossed paths in their development with other races. Between the existing races, it is not possible to find the simple relation of parent races to children races. Like the fibers in the network of a bath sponge, the tangle of the human races reflects a manifold, reciprocal connection. However, this is precisely what makes a simple genealogical arrangement impossible. From this point of view, what often seems peculiar – namely, that a race has primal relations from numerous sides – is self-evident.

★ ★ ★ ★

RACE CROSSING AND ITS CONSEQUENCES

The same racists who deem primitive history to be "an outstanding national science"[6] – who already concede in the titles of their books that they are pursuing political objectives: These same racists also preach the dogma about the necessity of the purity of the noble race and of the harmfulness and therefore abjection of miscegenation. Now, it is clear that racial mixing in a society founded on racial privileges makes maintaining these privileges more difficult. It increases the number of the privileged, blurs the line against the disenfranchised races, and equalizes the oppressed races with the master race. If the representatives of the master race rejected racial mixing for political reasons, for the sake of maintaining their undiminished prerogatives, it would be honest and one would know where one stood. However, they barricade themselves, as at an earlier time, behind the precepts of religion that does not even allow the Brahman to touch the pariah, let alone comingle with him. Today, this occurs behind the alleged teachings of science. Natural science and history show – so they claim – that the racial hybrid is physically and mentally inferior and that crossing generally leads to racial degeneration and eventual racial extinction.

In order to examine these allegations, it is necessary to subject the body of facts that modern science has accumulated on racial crossing and its results to an objective examination. If we want to determine through experiment the laws of crossing in plants and animals, then we would assume that there are pure breeds, i.e. groups that are uniform in their characteristics and predispositions. Such pure races, however, do not exist at all among humans, as every human race is the product of numerous, often ancient crossings. Even isolated racial splinter groups, like the small South American Indian tribe studied by [Theodor] Koch-Grünberg [1872–1924] along these lines, show

---

6   Gustaf Kossinna, *Die deutsche Vorgeschichte — eine hervorragend nationale Wissensschaft* [*The German History: A Superb National Science*] (Leipzig: Curt Kabitzsch, 1912), 4th ed., 1923.

such a diversity in the formation of the skull, nose, hair, disposition, etc. that the bastard nature is unmistakable. Thus, the popular evocation in the daily political struggle of a pure race cannot be taken seriously from the standpoint of biology. The opinion is also unfounded that buttresses the racial ideology that there were once pure races and that debased races only arose later due to miscegenation. Races, in fact, already mixed in primitive times; crossing was always an important factor in their development. In particular, every race that has undergone its own history and has major migrations in its past is the product of multiple racial mixtures.

With respect to humans, we speak of a crossing if the parents are distinguished from each other by a larger number of characteristic features for a particular race, by so-called "race-forming trait complexes." Nonetheless, even given this precondition, the delimitation of the term "crossing" is not always easy. Certainly, the comingling of a blond northern European male and a female Negro or Hottentot is to be regarded as a crossing. But, what about the union of a large, blond, long-headed German male and a small, brown-haired, round-headed female compatriot? Moreover, it is also rather customary to designate the connection between an "Aryan" male and a Jewish woman a crossing. . . .

A clear indication of the close relationship of all human races and the unity of humankind is the fact of mutual sexual attraction. Sexual attraction goes unabated between all human races where custom is not stronger than nature. . . .

But neither the language of hard facts nor logical thought prevent the racists from repeatedly preaching the ruinous nature of racial mixing and the need for maintaining racial purity. [Ludwig] Woltmann[7] [1871–1907], a follower of Gobineau and an opponent of Marxism, who, however, calls himself a socialist – in truth his views coincide most with those of today's Nazis – and is therefore someone that racists like to cite as a key witness, writes, for instance, in his *Political Anthropology*: "...the most superior human type, the fair North

---

7   Ludwig Woltmann, *Politische Anthropologie* [*Political Anthropology: A Study on the Influence of the Theory of Evolution in the Doctrine of the Political Development of Peoples*] (Leipzig: Thüringische, 1903), p. 112.

European race, is the most susceptible to crossing with colored races. Even the mixture with the brachycephalic [broad, short skull] and Mediterranean brown type must be considered ruinous in the long run. Moreover, these crossings, especially with homo brachycephalus (= Alpine, South German breed, author's note) appear after intensive mixing to lead to infertility and organic degeneration, as is most likely indicated by tooth decay and myopia ..." The "socialist" Woltmann works for the racists today insofar as he resorts to crutch words like "appear" and "most likely" to support, as evidence for his views, unproven and arbitrary allegations. He then continues: "It is no coincidence that [Georges Vacher de] Lapouge [1854–1936] compared the chaos of forms and colors of the Central European population, albeit somewhat exaggeratedly, to the racial chaos in the mixture of stray dogs. Here, Lapouge and Woltmann once again take up the popular comparison of human races to the breeds of canines. According to this view, "mutt people" (*Köter-Menschen*) arise from racially mixed people. (Of course, every dog connoisseur knows that mutts are certainly not to be considered inferior as a breed of canine with respect to resilience, intelligence, and loyalty.) And, it is only by maintaining the purity of the race that it is allegedly possible to achieve racially "noble" people.

The comparison, however, is misleading for two reasons. The noble race of silken pinschers and the noble race of the Greeks are two very different notions. The more a pet corresponds to a unnatural, human purpose, the more "noble" it is. In high-performance breeding, the hypertrophy of one or several traits desired by the breeder is obtained at the expense of the biological equilibrium. The "high-noble" English bacon pig has a potbelly and suffers from a fatty heart and dementia; it is only considered "noble" because its bacon rind provides a benefit to humans. We will thus call a human being and a human race noble when they are adapted to their environment in terms of all of their characteristics and the inclination of their own survival – when they are physically and mentally healthy and "gifted" in general. And when only healthy dispositions are combined, adaptability will be increased, not decreased, as a result of miscegenation.

The "pure breeding of blond individuals," which the racist side always puts forward as an ideal, is thus a rather preposterous utopia. In reality, the demand for keeping the race pure is only superficially a eugenic one; lurking behind it is the political and economic demand to restrict all new rivals from the racial privileges. The struggle against miscegenation is being waged by all those who wish to maintain the gap between the races, who demand for their own noble race a "*numerus clausus.*" When the "precise" naturalist and racist Lenz asserts, without being able to provide any scientific evidence, that "German-Jewish intermarriage contradicts both the interest of the Germanism and Judaism...," when the circumspect, genteel Jesuit and racist [Hermann] Muckermann [1877–1962] claims, also without any scientific justification, that "one may advocate for the most discreet possible preservation of the purity of the major races that make up the nations of the earth," they encounter the Jewish racists [Benjamin] Disraeli [1804–1881] and Ignaz Zollschan [1877–1944], who disapprove of miscegenation, because they fear that it could harm the "chosen people" with regard to their chosenness.

Yet, it is precisely the Jews, whose outstanding cultural activity has been witnessed throughout the history of the last several thousand years, that modern research has recognized as a mixed race. By the same token, the hybrid character of all races responsible for creating advanced cultures has long been proven. Anthropological research shows that precisely those areas have the highest level of miscegenation where human culture has reached the highest stage: We cite the Near East and India, North Africa and, above all, Europe, whose achievements have always been borne by a strongly racially mixed population. The German people of the past centuries represent a mixture of no less than 10 racial types (Nordic, "Dalic," Mediterranean, Alpine, Dinaric, Ostic, Aryan, Oriental, Asiatic, Near Eastern, Mongolian, Negro): "All of the above leads to the conclusion that in Germany, as in all of Europe, most people are of mixed race," writes even [Hans F.K.] Günther [1891–1968], the racist leader. And yet, the achievements of the German people have never been so vast and impressive as in the present period of its greatest interbreeding (*Zerkreuzung*).

Since the beginning of human history, it has especially been in the wake of war that racial crossing has asserted itself. Out of the unions between the conquerors and the women of the conquered – who may have been incorporated into the community as wives or slaves – a new current of life emerged. Frequently, the conquerors established a protective barrier for their racial privileges by means of caste systems. But the caste was only effective economically and politically – by hindering the rise of the oppressed into the conqueror race, which was also the ruling class – not biologically. This is because neither caste nor religion was able to prevent the rulers' lustful desire to mix their blood with that of the women from the people. It was even possible that the conqueror race in the foreign setting was subsequently absorbed by the local race. Military victory did not have to be biological.

In the present, the situation is no different. [World War I] soon brought prisoners, then occupying forces of all races into every European country; neither isolation, nor prejudices could prevent the racial mixing. For their part, the German imperialists who bemoaned the "black shame" certainly would have had no qualms about using colonial troops anywhere they could, if they had had the opportunity. In France, where the imperialist politicians have no greater fear than deterioration of the population, garrisons of Negro troops were nothing unusual, even in peacetime. In his essay "The Invasion of the Coloreds in Europe," [Hans] Harmsen[8] [1899–1989] criticizes the French racial policy: "The 'race of the future,' the ideal of mixed White and Colored that is now repeatedly defended by the French, means the deliberate transformation of the white population living in Europe today into a mixed race." He does not mention, however, that it is French chauvinists and nationalists who, with this certainly dubious ideal, want to achieve the same thing as the German chauvinists and nationalists with their equally dubious ideal of the Nordification (*Vernordung*) of the German people: The assertion of privilege.

At present, the most powerful states – America, England, France, Germany – are borne by a racially very mixed population. We would therefore do well to evaluate the allegations of racist historians – who tend to attribute the downfall of all great cultures, peoples and states to miscegenation, to "racial chaos" – with the necessary precaution. The notion that "racial chaos" inevitably leads to racial degeneration and eventually racial death was taught

---

8   [Hans] Harmsen, "*Der Einbruch der Farbigen in Europa,*" ["The Collapse of the Colored People in Europe"], *Archiv für Rassen- und Gesellschafts-Biologie*, 19 (1927): 54–63.

by Gobineau, [Georges Vacher de] Lapouge, Woltmann, and Chamberlain, and continues to be taught by their disciples Günther, Lenz, and others. According to Chamberlain, the racial mixing of Romans with emancipated Orientals and Negroes pulled down the noble Roman people into a "raceless chaos" and, finally, led to the downfall of the powerful Roman state. Similar to the end of Rome, Günther even attributes Greece's demise to the "drying up of Nordic blood," despite the fact that proportion of Nordic blood in the people of classical antiquity has been inferred on the basis of highly uncertain and highly unobjective hypotheses.

In truth, it was primarily economic and political causes that brought about the downfall of the Roman state. Only states have a natural death; races and peoples, on the other hand, disappear, but their genetic and cultural heritage remains, if only partly. The importation of slaves originating from the Rome's imperialist wars caused peasant labor to become more and more detached from slave labor. The free peasants moved to the city and became urban citizens. At the same time, large-land ownership, the "*latifundia*" of the rich Romans, who lived a self-indulgent lifestyle in Rome, increased. The overexploitation of resources – which was pursued in the Roman colonies in the late imperial period in all directions, even with respect to "human material" – finally exhausted the possibilities of slave importation. To secure the development of the fields, it was necessary to turn free slaves into tenant farmers. But the serfs (coloni) succumbed to the double burden of rent and taxes. They eventually abandoned the land and ran away.

Opulent Rome was not in a position to provide the masses with any food, which gave rise to Rome's depopulation. Military service was too hard for the soft Romans, so the warring generals filled their armies with foreign (Germanic, Gallic, Asia Minor) mercenaries. In the end, Italy fell prey to the hordes of foreign, battle-ready mercenaries. Hence, the development of the economic and political situation was to blame for the fall of Rome, not miscegenation. Indeed, miscegenation even played a role in the early days of Rome: At that time, Romans and Samnites had united with the subjugated, probably "non-Aryan" Etruscans and Ligurians, without, however, the national strength being impaired. The story of Rome's demise due to miscegenation and racial chaos is one of many fairy tales we encounter again and again in the books of the racists. Never has miscegenation caused the downfall of a race. On the other hand, it has often been the primary cause in the development of new breeds; through felicitous combinations, it has often initiated the beginning of a new culture and the rise of a people.

THE DOWNFALL OF LOWER RACES

People die when they get old; human races, however, do not die of their own accord. Yet, even though biological racial mixing has never brought the downfall of a race, political mixing with the white "conqueror race" – the brutal violence of European colonial policy – has brought death to many weaker races. Whoever racks their brain today about the reasons for the extinction of the "primitive," "wild" races of Tasmanians, Australians, Indians, etc. can only be an ignoramus or a hypocrite. Anyone who deals with colonial history will recognize the truth of the harsh words that Charles [Wentworth] Dilke [1843–1911] used to characterize his Anglo-Saxon brethren in his *Greater Britain* [1868]. He calls them "a killing race." This aspersion, however, does not apply only to them. It equally applies to the Spaniards and the Portuguese; the French and the Belgians; the Italians and the Germans – to all those who brought the "light of culture" to their darker brothers and thereby blew out the flame of their existence.

It is the same gruesome tale of greed, cruelty, and hypocrisy on the part of the whites, and fear and agony and death on the part of the colored races: from the crimes perpetrated by the predatory Spaniards under Cortez against the Aztecs of Mexico and under Pizarro against the Incas of Peru and their rich cultures, to the brutality of the English colonists in Tasmania and Australia, the Dutch governors in Insulindia, the Belgian government in Congo, and the German colonial generals in Southwest Africa. Wherever whites raided areas that, until then, were in the possession of a colored population, their only thought was to quickly occupy the land and its treasures. They reached their destination directly by expelling, enslaving, and killing the natives – under a quickly discovered pretext – or indirectly by cheating the people out of their possessions with shoddy goods, weakening them with alcohol and imported diseases, and making them docile with the missionaries they brought along.

The work that the pious Catholic Spaniards had begun on the high cultures of the Aztecs and Incas was completed by the devout puritanical British and Americans on the free hunter tribes of the North American Indians. [George]

Catlin[9] [1796–1872], an American painter who lived among American Indians from 1832 to 1840, related the story of their downfall in a startling book. In 1803, to the southeast of Australia, England began to colonize the island of Tasmania, which was populated by the unique primitive race of Tasmanians. The last of their tribe, the female "Truganini, whom the colonists flippantly and tastelessly called "Lala Rakh,"[10] died in 1876.

In 73 years, the time of a human life, the "higher" race managed to wipe the unfortunate "lower" race off the face of the earth. Actual hunts for natives were only one of the means by which this objective could be achieved so quickly. The representatives of the superior European race were deported criminals who had been brought from England to Tasmania and could now unleash their baser instincts on the defenseless "savages." While Australians, the related race on the continent, have not been fully eradicated, the small number of surviving representatives of the race only come into question any longer for expositions and museums. If the primitive dwarf peoples, the Akkas, Negritos, among others, still exist, it is merely because, to their benefit, they inhabit areas that are difficult for Europeans to access. Likewise, the Polar peoples (Eskimos, Tschukschten, and others) would have been decimated long ago if the areas they inhabit were more enticing for whites.

The fact that the brutal treatment of "colored peoples" is not necessarily a thing of the past can be seen from the modern colonial literature. We learn this, moreover, from the disturbing report that the Secretary of the General German Trade Union Federation, [Franz Josef] Furtwängler [1894–1965], presented to a commission of the League of Nations in Geneva on June 3, 1929 about a research trip undertaken to the tropics on behalf of the trade union confederation. Furtwängler told of the barbaric treatment of Indian workers; of the 300,000 suffering plantation coolies in the Dutch colonies; he further reported on the 25,000 Negroes who died like cattle in the construction of railway lines in French Congo; he told of the mandate of Ruanda Urundi, entrusted to the Belgians, which is called the "land of skeletons" and where

9   Catlin, G., *Die Indianer Nordamerikas,*" Reprint (Berlin: Sommerfeld, 1925).

10   Friedrich Ratzel, *Völkerkunde* [Ethnology] (Leipzig: Bibliographisches Institut, 1894).

60,000 people perished last year alone; he mentioned the telling provision of Portuguese colonial law, according to which pregnant Negro women in the six month of pregnancy may not be whipped. And the congress against colonial oppression – which, for the first time, brought together representatives of the freedom movement of all races from around the globe in Egmont Palace in Brussels in the summer of 1926 – "was like a fiery beacon, like a flash of lightning that announces an approaching storm from afar." (Magnus Hirschfeld, *Geschlechtskunde* II, 1928, p. 621.)

The work on the history of the kicked at and down trodden races and nations that is still missing today will be one of the most revolutionary books. Certainly, there is enough material – we could cite a long list of works that depict and condemn the oppression and destruction of "colored" people. We can see from this that the injustice and wickedness that Europe and America have committed against the weaker, not inferior races, has been well recognized by thousands and hundreds of thousands. At the same time, this knowledge is powerless against the greed of capitalist society, powerless against the cruelty and cold-bloodedness of chauvinistic imperialism. Only the victory of socialism will put a reasonable, humane planned economy with people in the place of a brutal policy of extermination – of course, for the primitive races, who still contribute to the colorfulness of the earth's racial mixture, it will then be too late.

There are no inferior races per se. Just as we fight against the privileges of the nobility for individual people, we likewise cannot concede the privilege of the nobility to individual races. By the same token, we take the view of the theory of evolution. We, therefore, must distinguish lower and higher human races in the sense that the former is closer to the original human tribe, the latter further removed. But evolutionary significance says nothing about physical or moral significance. It makes no sense to consider the "race" of dolphins to be more "valuable" than the "race" of salmon, because the former is higher up in the bloodline of the animal kingdom. It is true that the Nordic race bears today the most complex human culture. But every researcher who has studied the life of primitives has found that they are certainly not inferior people, yet, at the same time, usually happier than us whites. [Wilhelm] Schmidt [1868–1954] tells us this in reference to the Pygmies, [Wilhelm] Koppers [1886–1961] to the

Fuegians, and [Leo Victor] Frobenius [1873–1938], [Felix von] Luschan [1854–1924], [Karl] Weule [1864–1926], et al. to the Negroes.

The fact that one race is currently powerful and capable of suppressing others is no proof of its higher value. And, when the powerful search for pretexts to oppress and eradicate the weak, to give their violence the veneer of appropriateness by means of a "scientific" determination, science should not lend itself to such an end. It is true that the physical image of primitive peoples often does not give the impression of joyful strength and sinewy beauty, true that their mental life appears dull and crude to the casual observer. But let us consider the extraordinary stress, the arduous strains with hunger, cold and heat and constant danger under which primitives live, and how, then, his life conditions become even worse when whites enter into his circle of life as a disruptive force! If a colored human being finds a good environment and good care, the beauty of his body develops. It also evident that his mental abilities hardly lag behind those of a European.

The rigors of the harsh natural environment quickly deplete the body of the primitives and tread heavily on their intellect. But what have the proud rulers of humanity done to the poor of their own race, to the European proletariat, with the artificial milieu they have constructed? What have they done with the bodies of the exploited classes of Europe; with the men and women and children, who grow up in airless and lightless caverns, without adequate food and are tortured by scrofula and tuberculosis; with the spirit of European proletarians, who atrophy in the monotony of factory work? The primitive man in the thorny underbrush of the forest, on the edge of the sandy desert, in the interminable snows of the north – he is still a good deal happier than the European and American proletariat. Isolated from nature, the latter certainly does not know its dangers, but neither does he know its joys; he lives out his gray life within the gray walls of the city. The primitive man is happier in all his distress and danger, because he knows the excitement of the hunt and the joy of collecting and finding; he is happier because, as long as the noble white race does not enslave him, he is free.

But, today, slavery no longer exists – in the bourgeois democracies of Europe and America, the people are simply free and equal. "In ancient times, before democracy was invented," writes Karl in *Stine Menschenkind*,[11] "it was necessary to provide for the slaves, even if you had no use for them. But then the Americans, who are thoroughly versed in modern labor issues, find out that it's not worth it. And so they discovered freedom. . . ." The Negroes in the southern states are therefore now no longer slaves, even though the Klu Klux Klan regularly lynches some of them to remind them that they used to be. The millions of brown Hindus are no longer slaves, nor are the millions of yellow Chinese. Nonetheless, they have become proletarians – victims of capitalism, more defenseless than slaves and unhappier. When one reads about how women and children in India and China languish, day and night, in forced labor, about how thousands upon thousands die of hunger there each year, then one remembers the gruesome images from the factory that served as a torch for the despairing European proletariat, illuminating his own distress, that sparked the proletarian revolution in Europe. One recalls [Friedrich Engels] "The Condition of the Working Class in England [1845]." And for all of them – for the large races that have not yet been eradicated by the wanton destruction of whites, for all the "colored people" – a variation of the words of Karl Marx [1818–1883] holds: "The emancipation of the oppressed races can only be the work of the oppressed races themselves." This work, which [Mahatma] Gandhi [1869–1948] and Sun Yat-sen [1866–1925] have started, will be concluded by others. Then, when the colored races will have shown that they are not weaker, the ideology of racism will have no choice but to admit that they are not inferior. And then, perhaps, the way will have been cleared for an objective, non-evaluative racial science.

---

11 [Martin] Andersen Nexø, *Stine Menschenkind* [*Stine Man*] (Munich: A. Langen, 1919/1921), p. 679.

RACE IN SCIENCE AND POLITICS

Excerpts

By Hugo Iltis

Translated from the German by Kareem James Abu-Zeid, PhD

German edition: *Rasse in Wissenschaft und Politik*

Prague: Wahrheit, 1935

RACISM IN THE MANTLE OF SCIENCE

The myth of blood is being proclaimed in Germany. Blood—rather than humanity and solidarity, as we believe—is said to bind men together. The smell of blood is on the rise: similarly to what happened in the Middle Ages with the belief in witches, tens of thousands of innocent people are now being sacrificed to the belief in race. Racism teaches that the human races are of different worth, that the "Aryan" or Nordic race singlehandedly—or almost singlehandedly—founded human culture, that race determines the great movements in history, and that race is the "engine of history."

A hundred years ago, when European imperialism was beginning to stir its limbs, the ideas of modern racism were first announced, in the form of novels or essays, by [Benjamin] Disraeli [1804–1881], the English Jew, and by [Joseph Arthur, Comte de] Gobineau [1816–1882], the French count. While Disraeli, the Jew, assigned the status of a noble race to the Jewish race in addition to the Germanic one, Gobineau, the French aristocrat, recognized the northern French nobility, the descendants of the old Normans, as the bearers of the best race. From the teachings of its very first representatives, we can already recognize the nature of racist ideology: every racist sees the ideal in his own race. Racism has nothing to do with science and reason—it is nothing other than a political method for securing the primacy of one's own race.

In prewar Germany, the works of the Englishman [Houston Stewart] Chamberlain [1855–1827], who wrote in German, had a profound influence on the thought and actions of the German aristocracy and bourgeoisie. Kaiser Wilhelm II was in the habit of gifting his friends sumptuously bound copies of the *Foundations of the 19th Century* [1899]. In order to have the Germanic race shine more brightly, Chamberlain chose the Jewish "race" as a dark backdrop and announced a somewhat camouflaged and theoretical—but all the more effective—anti-Semitism. The careful way he dealt with this topic was a result of the fact that the title page of his *Foundations* bears a dedication to the Jewish botanist [Julius von] Wiesner [1838–1916].[1] Making use of the "preliminary work" of [Ludwig] Woltmann [1871–1907] and others, Chamberlain sought to prove the Germanic descent of all the great men of the European nations—Dante, Michelangelo, and also Napoleon. He even made an Aryan of Christ, who, like all of his heroes, is said to be blond. Through ingratiating and tasteless self-praise of the Germanic race, Chamberlain's books have implanted an excessive self-confidence—that belief in the "German mission," in the "German spirit that shall heal the world"[2]—in broad circles of Germany's ruling classes, helping create the atmosphere that led to the World War.

In the war Germanic Englishmen fought against Germanic Germans—blood did not prove thicker than water. Nevertheless, in postwar Germany racism rose to ever-prouder heights. After the defeat in reality, a part of the German petty bourgeoisie and intellectuals, namely, the youth, looked for compensations in fantasy. While the earlier racists were men of letters, people were now, in the age of the natural sciences, trying to provide scientific proofs of racism with pseudo-scientific, biological arguments. [Hans F. K.] Günther's [1891–1968] books became the gospel of the racist community. Before we take up Günther's work and method, we would like to take a look at the facts of objective science that pertain to human races.

Anthropologists distinguish a small number of major races or racial circles of humanity. In my work *Popular Race Theory* (Jena 1930), I divide humanity into five major races: the Australid, the Pygmaeid, the Negrid, the Mongolid, and the Europid. In his recently published large work *Race Theory and Race History of Humanity*[3] [Egon Freiherr von] Eickstedt [1892–1965] distinguishes only three large major races: the Negrid, with which he combines the Australid; the Mongolid, with the Indianid minor race; and the Europid. But there are

---

1   Translator's note: Julius Ritter von Wiesner.

2   Translator's note: A reference to the political slogan (originally from a poem by Emanuel Geibel) *Am deutschen Wesen mag die Welt genesen* ("The world will be healed by the German spirit").

3   Egon Freiherr von Eickstedt, *Rassenkunde und Rassengeschichte der Menschheit* (Stuttgart: F. Enke, 1934).

countless transitional stages between these major races, so that a sharp divide by either physical or psychological qualities does not seem possible. All the same, it should be possible to draft not only a physical but also a psychological character image for the typical representatives of the major races—but *only* for these races! A valuation of these major races in relationship to one another is no longer a matter of science, however. The Negroes are very good musicians, and they have proven themselves to be the most outstanding athletes at the Olympic Games. In Japan, the Mongols have founded the most modern military power. Each race has its own special features—how one values them is a matter of taste and not the task of science.

With its valuations, neo-German racism does not limit itself to the large major races of humanity; rather, its value judgments occur in relation to sub-races within the Europid major strain. Even [Johann Friedrich] Blumenbach [1752–1840], the founder of modern race theory, did not distinguish any sub-races within the Europid major race. [William Z.] Ripley [1867–1941] later distinguished three European racial types [*The Races of Europe*, 1899]: the Nordic or Teutonic, the Alpine, and the Mediterranean. In my *Popular Race Theory*, I distinguish the following racial types within the European racial mixture: the Nordic; the Mediterranean, together with the closely related Oriental; the Dinaric, together with the related Armenoid; and finally the Alpine and the Ostic.

Eickstedt asserts almost the same racial elements within the European population. He also puts forward a Turanid type, which I consider an Alpine-Mongolian mixed type, as well as an Indid type, which I take to be a mixed type between the Oriental and the Dravidian race that originally lived in India.

The population of Europe, including the German people, is composed of these racial types. Within the population of Germany, the Nordic, the Alpine, the Dinaric, and the Ostic types are the most common. There is no "German race"; the German people represent an extremely racially mixed population. Similarly, European or German Jews also demonstrate a diverse racial composition. With them too, it is only the sub-races of the Europid major race that play a role, namely, the Oriental element (which is closely related to the Mediterranean), the Armenid element (which is related to the Dinaric and is linked to it through transitional stages), but also, especially in Central and Eastern Europe, the Nordic, Alpine, and Ostic elements. The Jews are thus in no way a foreign race in Europe—one would then also have to declare the population of Southern Europe to be foreign to Europe, for it demonstrates a very similar racial composition!

The population of Europe and the Near East is composed of the aforementioned five to nine types, to which the Mongolid or the Negrid admixtures are occasionally appended. But pure racial types are exceptions. The vast majority of these people demonstrate a diverse mixture of features, forming an utterly hybridized population. Every Mendelist knows how complicated and diverse a human population always becomes if it arises through the crossbreeding of racial types that differ in numerous independently hereditary characteristics.

From the Europid racial mixture, the anthropological science has singled out the aforementioned racial types—which can be distinguished by their physical characteristics—in order to facilitate orientation. It must also be recognized that certain psychological characteristics are related to certain physical features. However, science has not yet, in any way, been able to demonstrate how certain psychological features are linked to certain physical features of the Europid type, nor has it been able to demonstrate that these two are linked to one another in any way at all. Blond men are no better, no cleverer, and no braver than brunettes. Among the great men of history, there are just as many—and perhaps even more—people with round skulls as there are people with long skulls; and in addition to people with large bodies there are also people with small bodies, such as Kant, Beethoven, Napoleon, etc. And certain psychological features are just as unlikely to be definitively linked to individual racial features as they are to be definitively linked to certain Europid racial types. It cannot be proven that members of the Nordic racial type are healthier than members of the Alpine racial type: all illnesses—cancer, tuberculosis, mental illnesses, etc.—occur just as frequently in Northern Europe, where the Nordic racial type is settled, as they do in Central Europe. Similarly, it cannot be proven that the Nordic race is any more moral than the Mediterranean race or the Oriental race, for example. The courts in Sweden and Norway convict blond Nordics of the same offenses of which the courts in Italy convict dark-haired Mediterraneans. If certain differences do exist, then these are much more determined by the diversity of climates and lifestyles than by racial peculiarities. Similarly, there is just as little evidence that the intellectual and artistic achievements of the various European racial types are significantly different from one another in terms of their respective values.

The neo-German scientific racism founded by Hans F.K. Günther [1891–1968] and his followers, as well as the entire field of "scholarly" anti-Semitism, are founded on just such a valuation of the psychological capacities of individual racial elements within the European racial mixture.

Günther, a former high school teacher and a philologist by training, is the author of the racist Günther community's "holy books." His *Race Theory of the German People*[4] went through numerous editions in just a few years. This work, along with Günther's other racial picture books, which the Lehmann press in Munich has been reproducing in these favorable economic conditions, became the gospel of the "educated" German youth and significantly influenced their mentality. Whoever had read Günther was ripe for the reading of *Mein Kampf*.

Günther has a very skillful method of propaganda. Through photographs that were supposedly chosen at random, he establishes not only the race but also the various "racial impacts" of the people depicted. As examples of the sympathetic races, namely, the Nordic race, he provides beautiful and well-coiffed heads from the upper strata of society; as examples of the "unsympathetic races," such as the Alpine or the Jewish races, the selection is less favorable. For Europe and also Germany, Günther puts forward the same racial elements that we mentioned above—although he unnecessarily gives some of these types new names. Yet Günther not only knows which *physical* qualities each of these races has; he also knows which psychological qualities— and what level of cultural achievement and cultural significance—are inherent to each racial type. He thus analyzes the German racial chaos in its elements and then hands out grades ranging from "excellent" to "unsatisfactory" to each racial component according to his whims—he was a high school teacher, after all. The Nordic race naturally receives a grade of "excellent"; the Dinaric and Mediterranean races are qualified as "satisfactory"; and the Alpine and

---

4   Hans F.K. Günther, *Rassenkunde des deutschen Volkes* (Munich: Lehmann, 1930).

Jewish races are qualified as "unsatisfactory." Most of the population of central France and central Germany, Switzerland, Czechoslovakia, and Poland belong to the Alpine race. Günther names the Alpine race the "Ostic," for according to his—very unproven—hypothesis, that race "seeped in" to Europe from Asia and brought democracy to Europe and Germany as an evil Asian legacy, one that Günther hates like the plague. Half of Germany has already been "easternized," and Günther sees deliverance in promoting the propagation of the Nordic race and in the creation of a Nordic Internationale.

Official German science has benevolently promoted Güntherian pseudo-scientific racism. Only a few voices have been raised against this irruptive intellectual epidemic. "I accuse this book of a crime against the intellectual life of the German people," writes Dr. [Friedrich] Merkenschlager [1892–1968], a lecturer at the University of Kiel, who sees the crime of the Güntherian book in "that it strives to put millions of good and excellent Germans into the dungeon of inferior race and cut them off from the light." Merkenschlager's warning was no use. Racism as a theory continued to feed hungrily, like an insidious fever—until all of a sudden the illness became acute, and the swelling bulge of practical, political racism burst open. The events in Germany have shown the world what a dangerous poison racism is for the nation or people infected by it. Racism should be considered a contagious disease in the present time of enormous crisis, in this time of fierce struggle for the existence of individuals and peoples. It is essential to immunize the people against it as against a contagious disease.

RACISM: INTELLECTUAL POISON GAS

Writing under the pseudonym "Dr. Wolf Bodansky"[5]

The science of the human races, which takes as its goal knowledge of the facts and research into the truth, provides no foundations whatsoever for the claim that we have only certain individual human races to thank for the emergence of human culture, and that there are worthless races in addition to worthy ones. The racism that puts forward these claims is no science and has nothing to do with science—it is nothing other than a malicious and dangerous weapon for political struggle. This is acknowledged in present-day Germany. There, it has been officially proclaimed that science's primary significance should be to benefit the nation—it is not supposed to be objective, but rather consciously subjective and national. "Also in science the folkish state has to see a means for the promotion of national pride," we read in *Mein Kampf* (12th edition, p. 473/635[6]). "Instinctive" myth has taken the place of objective science.

With citations from the two major works of German political racism, it will be shown how the racial politicians make use of this lethal weapon, this

---

5   Translator's note: This essay, the last in the book *Race in Science and Politics*, was clearly written by Hugo Iltis, although it was published under a pseudonym. Whole paragraphs of this essay are virtually identical (with minor changes) to passages in Iltis' 1936 book *The Myth of Blood and Race.*

6   Translator's note: For all quotations from *Mein Kampf,* unless otherwise noted, I am using the English version produced by John Chamberlain et al.: *Mein Kampf: Complete and Unabridged.* Editorial sponsors: John Chamberlain, et al. Reynal & Hitchcock, New York 1941. It is available online at: https://archive.org/stream/meinkampf035176mbp/meinkampf035176mbp_djvu.txt.
The page numbers given throughout refer first to the German original that Iltis cites, and then to the English version (i.e., German/English). I have occasionally modified the translation very slightly to bring it closer to the original German.

"intellectual poison gas," against all peoples and human groups that they want to kill either economically or politically.

In Hitler's *Mein Kampf* (we are citing the 12th edition, Munich 1932, which was published before Hitler's coup), racism is the foundation on which the entire worldview is based. "The race question," we read on page 372/470, "not only furnishes the key to world history, but also to human culture as a whole." And on page 421/581, the author writes: "In this world human culture and civilization are inseparably bound up with the existence of the Aryan. His dying-off or his decline would again lower upon this earth the dark veils of a time without culture."

Science, even national science, unconditionally refuses to use the term "Aryan" in relation to race. This term merely unites a group of different languages—there are Aryan languages, but there is no Aryan race. Even Hans F. K. Günther [1891–1968] writes, in his *Race Theory of the German People*[7] (15th edition, p. 358): "The designation 'Aryan' has now become scientifically unusable, and one is urgently advised against its application." Consequently, terms such as "Aryan descent" and "Aryan paragraph" are utterly meaningless.

According to Günther, the German people are composed of seven major races and five minor races—but primarily of an obviously diverse mixture of these twelve racial types. In *Mein Kampf*, we read the following (p. 728/935): "The foreign policy of a national state is charged with guaranteeing the existence on this planet of the race embraced by the state...." Where in Germany is there "the race embraced by the state"? The German people are a mixture of very different racial types. Are all of these races "Aryan"? These same racial elements also comprise the other peoples of Europe, including the Jewish people group—one would thus, logically, also have to consider the Jews to be Aryans. But logic plays no role in racism. In the parlance of National Socialist politics, Aryan is simply everything that is not Jewish. A racist will become embarrassed if he is asked about the race of the American Indians. The Indians are not Jews—so they must be Aryans!

---

7   Hans Friedrich Karl Günther, *Rassenkunde des deutschen Volkes* (Munich: Lehmann, 1930).

We note the following: There is no Aryan race, nor has there ever been one—the German people are a mixture of different racial types, an utterly hybridized population—and yet the entire worldview developed in *Mein Kampf* is based on the superiority of this non-existent Aryan race and on the non-existent blood ties of the German people.

The fact that the German people, despite their mixed race and hybridization, exhibit the greatest achievements in all domains somehow provides absolutely no reason for racism to approve of racial mixing and hybridization—for logic is of no consequence to racism. Instead, racial mixing is declared a crime, is declared "blood defilement." "Peoples that bastardize themselves, or permit themselves to be bastardized, sin against the will of eternal providence" (*Mein Kampf*, p. 359/452). "The loss of the purity of blood alone destroys inner happiness forever; it eternally lowers man, and never again can its consequences be removed from body and mind" (p. 359/452). These grand dogmas put forth with such certainty about the consequences of miscegenation, of "racial defilement," as they are tastefully named in the Third Reich, make only one mistake: they contradict the facts established by science. Eugen Fischer [1874–1967], the director of the Kaiser Wilhelm Institute in Berlin and the first rector of the University of Berlin under the National Socialist regime—therefore certainly an unsuspicious witness!—not only determined in his famous studies on the Rehoboth Basters that a physically and mentally capable hybrid people emerged even from the crossbreeding of Dutch people and Hottentots—two certainly very different races. He also, shortly before Hitler's coup (in early 1933), summarized our general knowledge of miscegenation in a presentation at the Kaiser Wilhelm Society and determined that, at least as far as Germany is concerned, the highest artistic and scientific achievements were and still are by racially mixed people. Even the racist Günther stresses that men like Luther, Goethe, Beethoven, etc.—the spiritual leaders of the nation!—were in no way of pure race, and still less of pure Nordic race. And today, now that the search for non-Aryan grandmothers is in vogue, one is astonished to hear that Paul Heyse [1830–1914], the great poet and Nobel laureate, [Adolf von] Baeyer [1835–1917], the great chemist and also a Nobel laureate, Hans von Marées [1837–1887], the great and genius painter, along with many others from among Germany's finest sons, all had German fathers and Jewish mothers—that they were products of "racial defilement"!

Despite the facts of the matter, which have been established by experience and by science, the entire political argument of racism is based on incorrect claims about the horrific effect of miscegenation. These claims were primarily used to defame France. The French are a Jewish-Negro hybrid people and are therefore inferior and degenerate:

Exactly for this reason France is, and remains by far, the most terrible enemy. This people, which is constantly becoming more negrofied, constitutes, by its tie with the aims of Jewish world domination, a grim danger for the existence of the European white race. For infection in the heart of Europe through Negro blood on the Rhine corresponds equally to the sadistic perverse vengefulness of this chauvinistic hereditary enemy of our people, and to the ice-cold plan of the Jews to begin bastardizing the European continent at its core.

What France, spurred by its own vengefulness, methodically led by the Jew, is doing in Europe today, is a sin against the existence of white humanity, and someday will inspire against that nation all the avenging spirits of a knowledge that will have recognized race pollution as the original sin against mankind.

For Germany, however, the French danger means an obligation to subordinate all considerations of sentiment, and to reach out the hand to those who, threatened as much as we are, will not tolerate and bear France's drive toward dominion" (*Mein Kampf*, p. 704–5/907–908).

Such quotations, whose number could be multiplied at will, show to what ends racism is used, and reveal its true face to us. And the same spirit of brutal mendacity also shines through the mess of hollow phrases in the large work by the theorist and foreign policy head of the Nazis—Alfred Rosenberg's [1893–1946] *The Myth of the 20th Century*.[8] According to Rosenberg—and we are citing from the third edition, Munich 1932—the French Revolution eradicated the best remnants of the noble Germanic master race of France. France was once blond and German, today it is degenerate. But a few blond Frenchmen must

---

8   Alfred Ernst Rosenberg, *The Myth of the Twentieth Century* [*Der Mythus des 20. Jahrhunderts*, 3rd ed. (München: Hoheneichen-Verlag, 1932)].

still be around, otherwise they would not have been able to win the World War.

In 1914, Germany faced this power of northern France, which was still strong (Normandy was always considered a 'small Germany' in the Middle Ages and beyond[9]). However, it was not prominent personalities with blood ties to the Germans who now had control over this power, but rather Rothschild bankers and other financial powers who were racially related to them. And with them people like Fallières, Millerand, or the Alpine impotence of Herriot and company. Thus it is only today that the last valuable blood is seeping away. Entire regions in the south have died out and are now drawing in the people of Africa, as Rome once did. An increasingly decaying population is flooding into Paris, around the Notre Dame. Negroes and mulattoes are linking arms with white women, a purely Jewish quarter is emerging with new synagogues. South American, mestizo-like posers are polluting the race of the still-beautiful women who are attracted to Paris from all over France. We are thus currently experiencing something that has already unfolded in Athens, Rome, and Persepolis.

Therefore a close relationship with France, to say nothing of the political-military aspect, is equivalent to a marriage with someone afflicted with the plague. The call here is rather for the following: isolation of the European West; border closures on account of anthropological features; a Nordic-European coalition; cleansing the European motherland of the germs of Africa and Syria that are spreading out from central France" (*Myth*, p. 118/119).

The man who is attacking France's honor in this way is no ordinary soldier of the Nazi army—he is the Third Reich's head of foreign policy. These quotations all clearly demonstrate the meaning of racist ideology. That ideology is a dangerous and malicious tool for denigrating and dealing with one's political and economic

---

9   Translator's note: The German text simply reads "in der Ketzerzeit" here, which literally means "in the age of heretics." It is not an expression I know of, but I believe it to be the Reformation movement within the Catholic Church (during the Renaissance), and possibly to the period prior to that (i.e., the Late Middle Ages), when no small number of heretics were being put to death.

opponents. Like France itself, France's allies of the time, the Czechs and Poles, are denied racial honor. Along these lines, Alfred Rosenberg's portrayal of Hussitism, or rather Taboritism, is typical. "... Taboritism cost the Czech nature virtually all the unique civilized powers it possessed. Since then, this people has been uncreative and owes its later cultural recovery to the recently inrushing German formal powers. To this day, savageness combined with cowardice remains a characteristic of the Czech nature (Hasek's 'Svejk' is the authentic national hero of this incompetent nation)." "This view of Czech history is extremely instructive for all subsequent racist historical research and teaches the sharp distinction between freedom and 'freedom.' [...] Attributing an external 'freedom' to Czechs, Poles, and Levantines today means surrendering oneself to racial chaos" (Alfred Rosenberg, *Myth*, p. 125 and 126).

In these quotations by Rosenberg we can recognize the "absolute, impudent, and unilateral stubbornness" (p. 201/238) that is recommended in *Mein Kampf* as an effective means of agitation. The Czechs are the nation of Komensky[10], the first "good European" and the great educator; they are the nation of [Thomas] Masaryk [1850–1837], the powerful revolutionary and president, the "philosopher on the throne"; they are the nation of [composers] [Bedřich] Smetana [1824–1884] and [Antonín Leopold] Dvořák [1841–1904], whose music belongs among the most noble of humanity's achievements. But according to Rosenberg, "savageness combined with cowardice" is "a characteristic of the Czech nature"—therefore it is madness to grant them their external freedom, i.e., their own state.

The quotations from *Mein Kampf* and from Rosenberg's *Myth* demonstrate what racism means. But we do not need to pick this out of quotations. The fate of the German Jews has shown to what ends racism is used. The German persecution of the Jews over the past few years is a warning for all peoples.

Every European should read Hitler's *Mein Kampf*. In these books, scorn is preached not only for the Jews. The great French nation as well, which has stood at the forefront of humanity in all its struggles, is labeled degenerate

---

10   Translator's note: Komensky is more commonly referred to as [John Amos] Comenius 1592–1670], Czech philosopher and theologian, in English.

and racially polluted—and the Czechs, Poles, Russians, etc. are also "dealt with" racially. The English and Italians are only exempted from the general scorn of all who are different because it is hoped that they can be used as tools. The peoples who know to protect themselves against armaments with armaments of their own must not forget to defend themselves against intellectual preparations for war as well. There is not much to add to the quotations from *Mein Kampf* and *The Myth of the 20th Century*. Let us defend ourselves against the intellectual poison gas of racism—before it's too late!

THE MYTH OF BLOOD AND RACE

By Hugo Iltis

Translated from the German by Kareem James Abu-Zeid, PhD

German edition: *Der Mythus von Blut und Rasse*

Vienna: Rudolf Harrand Press, 1936
German book cover designed by Hans Waloschek

FOREWORD

The belief that the truth will prevail by itself is an illusion. The violence of the spirit is subject to the spirit of violence when the people of spirit will not fight. The propaganda that is spreading like a toxic plume over Europe needs to be defeated by propaganda: book must be used against book, newspaper against newspaper, radio against radio, technology against technology. Nazi propaganda is not about truth or falsehood, right or wrong; it is only about achieving its political goal: power. "The Law is whatever benefits Germany." This brutal legal theory proclaimed by the champions of the "New Germany" necessarily leads not only to the suppression of all political, national, and religious minorities, but also to intellectual "autocracy," the elimination of each nation's mutual security, and, ultimately and most certainly, to war. Racism, the doctrine that only one's own race is noble while all others are inferior, provides the legal foundation for a vicious politics of repression and conquest. Everyone who yearns for peace and freedom in their own homes and in the world at large must defend themselves against this racism.

This small book calls for a struggle against racism. It is written in a popular style—it seeks to immunize the masses against the "intellectual poison gas" of racism that threatens them. However, it also addresses the representatives of science. By clearly revealing the consequences of the delusion of race to them, this book shows them that they have a sacred duty not to remain on the sidelines of this struggle. It is not enough to laugh at those who believe in race—subtle irony fails in the face of blind fanaticism and raging brutality. Anthropologists and biologists, historians and sociologists, academies and universities from every civilized nation—all must take a stand in this struggle over mankind's future and happiness, must offer resistance against the lie's advance, and must help the truth gain victory. Resistance research has already begun to be organized. A world court of international science will expose racism as a product of hatred and the lust for power, a product of fantasy and falsehood. Then mankind will be freed from this nightmare and can proceed toward organizing a happy future in a spirit of cooperation.

Brno, February 1936

Dr. Hugo Iltis

RACISM AND SCIENCE

Racism is the ideological foundation of German National Socialism. In the name of the doctrine of the one true race, people are stripped of their rights and tortured, laws of humanity are broken, and laws of brutality are issued and enforced. For decades, an industrious pseudoscience has propagated the idea of racism in Germany and thus laid the groundwork for the atmosphere of the "national revolution." In the following, we will attempt to contrast the factual material of objective science with the argumentation of pseudoscientific racism.

The existence of corporeally different human races is a fact. A blond Scandinavian, a Mongolian Tungus, and a black Sudanese person are types of people whose bodily differences are obvious. Race theory, a partial science within anthropology, has given itself the task of describing and differentiating the individual human races. This scientific race theory is fairly recent: its founders were Carl Linnaeus [1707-1778] and [Johann Friedrich] Blumenbach [1752-1840], [Pieter] Camper [1722-1789] and [Anders] Retzius [1796-1860]— researchers who lived some 100 to 150 ago. Race theory's field of work, that of systematic anthropology, must be separated from ethnology or the study of peoples [Völkerkunde], just as the two concepts of *race* and *Volk* ["people"] are conceptually separate. Under the term *race*, one understands a group of people who, through a common location, are distinguished by considerable bodily characteristics; under the term *Volk*, a people group who, through socially acquired psychological qualities, through a common culture and language, through history and fate, appear to be associated. The third concept, *nation*, would then be applied to a people or a people group as a political subject, as the bearer of a state or a state mentality.

For ages, the concepts of *Volk* and race have both only referred to primitive and isolated groups of people. The words "a *Volk*, a race!" thus apply to certain Pygmies, certain Australians, and Eskimos. In contrast, all large civilized peoples demonstrate an extraordinarily strong mixture of races, just as a certain large race can play a role in the most diverse of peoples.

There are, for example, Mongolian racial characteristics not only among Japanese and Chinese people, but also among Russians and Turks. The Mediterranean race appears not only among Spaniards and Italians, but also among Greeks and the English.

It is certainly wrong to completely deny the significance of the question of race, or to deny the existence of different human races. Perhaps one day someone, through a kind of "vocational aptitude test of the races," will succeed in establishing links between certain psychological qualities and certain bodily racial characteristics, and on the basis of this insight partially explain the cultural achievements of peoples by means of their racial compositions. We are nowhere near this today, however, and must therefore make a sharp distinction between the (bodily) concept of race and the (cultural) concept of *Volk*.

One must always keep in mind that each European people [*Volk*] in particular is composed of many races, and that almost every one of the racial types of the major European races can be linked—to a greater or lesser extent, or rather, in varying degrees—to all European peoples.

Yet despite this observation, the task of science remains the following: to establish, precisely describe, and distinguish as keenly as possible between the large race types of humanity as well as the various sub-races within the larger races. In the following, we will attempt to succinctly present the results of race theory, i.e., that branch of the natural sciences that has the task of describing and systematizing the human races.

Living humanity forms a single species, the species *Homo sapiens* or the "wise man," as Linnaeus named him with almost ironically appealing certainty. Within the human species, the human races assume roughly the same position that the races of domestic animals assume within a certain species of domestic animal. It is certain, for example, that within the species of the domestic dog (*Canis familiaris*) the races exhibit far greater differences among themselves than within the *Homo sapiens* species—consider a whippet, a poodle, a bulldog, etc. And yet they all belong to the same species, which primarily expresses the fact that they can mate with one another without impediment. Delineating the separate human races is much harder due to the large degree of racial mixing. For with people there is no breeder who is interested in racial purity. Indeed, as we shall later see, racial purity in humans is in no way an ideal. The systematics, or rather classifications, of the human races therefore vary according to the perspective adopted and according to the classifying principle on which the researcher bases his work. There are classifications that distinguish only three large human races, and there are classifications that pick out over one hundred racial types. The now outdated Blumenbachian classification is well known. It uses skin color to distinguish between the following races: the white or Caucasian race; the black or Ethiopian; the yellow or Mongolian; the brown or Malayan; and the red or Indian. Modern science divides humanity into a small number of major races or racial circles, which are then subdivided into a larger number of sub-races. In my book *Popular Race Theory* (*Volkstümlicher Rassenkunde*, Uraniaverlag, Jena 1930), I made use of the results of modern research to distinguish five large formal circles or major races, namely, the Australoid (Australians, etc.), the Pygmoid (dwarf races), the Nigritoid (Negroes, etc.), the Mongoloid (Mongolians, etc.), and the Europoid (Europeans, etc.) circles.[1] In the most recent classification, which Egon von Eickstedt provides in his *Race Theory and Racial History of Humanity* (*Rassenkunde und Rassengeschichte der Menschheit*, Encke, Stuttgart 1933), the three large major races or corporeal groupings—the Europid (the white race), the Negrid (the black race), and the Mongolid (the yellow race)—are retained, but the Indian race is detached from the Mongolid to form a fourth major race, while the Australid is combined with the Negrid, and the individual groups of Pygmid circles are divided among the three large major races.

In the following, we will provide a brief characterization of the individual major races.

I. The Australid race (Image 1) has certain features in common with the black race, and others in common with the white race. Their skin color is dark and their cranium long; their hair, however, is not woolly but rather curly;

---

1   Note: These sections are not included in the translation of *Volkstümlicher Rassenkunde* in this book.

their body is extremely hairy, in contrast to the Negro. It is the build of the skeleton, however, that justifies maintaining the Australid as a distinct major race. The cranium is particularly characteristic, with its sloping forehead, the strong formation of its eyebrow bulge, and the minor development of the chin—all qualities that demonstrate a pronounced resemblance to that specific prehistoric race from the Ice Age (Aurignac), so that we can consider the Australians and even more so the extinct Tasmanians as the most primitive living human races. All of the forms that belong here (Tasmanians, Australians, black inhabitants of the South Seas or Melanesians, among others) are either extinct or in the process of going extinct, or, more accurately, have been condemned to extermination by the more powerful, but not better, Europids—"White shadows!"

II. The same holds true for the peculiar formal circle of the dwarf races or Pygmies. All Pygmies are characterized by their diminutive height (140 to 155 cm) and their mostly childlike skeletons, as well as by the fact that they almost always live in so-called areas of retreat (primeval forests, deserts, etc.)— they were forced into such areas by the stronger large races. Incidentally, the individual races that are included herein demonstrate such great differences that one can understand why Eickstedt, for example, considers the South African Pygmies to belong to the black major race, the Veddas and the Ainu to belong to the white major race, and South Africa's Bushmen to belong to the yellow major race. According to [Egon Freiherr von] Eickstedt [1892–1965], the Pygmies do not constitute their own major race, but rather primitive and suppressed dwarf forms of the large races. In contrast, other researchers, such as the Catholic anthropologists [Wilhelm] Schmidt [1868–1964], [Paul] Schebesta [1887–1967], and [Wilhelm] Koppers [1886–1961], among others, consider the Pygmies to be a uniform and original branch of humanity.

The researchers who live among the Pygmies tell of their kind, childlike hearts and of their primitive but intimate family lives. The Pygmies have been named an ugly race. But even aside the fact that beauty and ugliness are relative concepts that depend on taste, the designation "ugly" still cannot be used, as it pertains to a European sense of taste in reference to certain Pygmies, such as the south Asian Senoi, for example. The ugliness of primitive tribes—of the Australians, the Akha[2], etc.—is often only the result of the miserable living conditions in which they find themselves. The proletarians of our own countries who suffer from hunger and tuberculosis and grow up in filth are not beautiful either—but this has nothing to do with race!

Just like the forms that belong to the Australid major race, the Pygmies are doomed to die out—their extinction is only a matter of time. The great white "brother" has done away with them, and the few that remain no longer have any significance for the history of our plant—at best, they still have some for its museums.

III. In contrast, the third large major race, the black, Nigritic, or Negrid race (Eickstedt), with well over 100 million individuals, constitutes a significant portion of the earth's population. Their home is the African continent. The African Negroes and their American Negro descendants constitute a relatively uniform race. Most of them have tall, lean builds (165–180 cm), long and slender limbs, and mostly narrow, long crania, thick lips, somewhat prominent mouths, broad noses, woolly hair, and dark brown-black skin with little hair. The Negroes, too, are often called an ugly race, but this is utterly wrong! The Negro body, in terms of the beauty of its build, can certainly be compared to that of the European race (Image 2). The beautiful Negro dancer Josephine Baker brought joy to Aryan and non-Aryan socialites young and old. Certain differences in the black populations of northern and central Africa can be attributed to racial mixing with European, or rather Near Eastern, elements, whereas in South Africa crossbreeding with Hottentots and Bushmen changed the race. Modern Abyssinians constitute such a Negrid-European crossbreed. Everyone will admit that the lovely Amhara girl in Image 3 and the beautiful masculine forms of the magnificent Abyssinian warriors in Image 4 are the best evidence of the fact that crossbreeding, and indeed the crossbreeding of two different major races, in no way necessarily lead to a poor result, and that

2   Translator's note: The German here was Äkka, a word that I could not find anywhere. "Akha" is my best guess for this term.

the racist doctrines of the terrible consequences of miscegenation are nothing more than idiotic fairytales.

The African Negroes have the broadest range of levels of culture, from the primitive levels of hunters and gathers to the powerful Negro states with agricultural populations and an upper class composed of warriors. The most recent research by [Leo] Frobenius [1873–1938] has have shown that truly high Negro cultures had developed in the heart of Africa, but that they must have collapsed with the encroaching of the white people. The Negroes of the United States are demonstrating that they are capable of working within white culture. The Negro Tuskegee University in Alabama is headed by a full-blooded Negro, Dr. Robert Russa Moton [1867–1940]. Many Negroes and mullatoes have earned academic degrees—there are Negro professors, Negro doctors, etc. Negro musicians and Negro athletes are winning awards and breaking records. The great actor Paul Robeson [1898–1976], the famous Negro tenor Roland Hayes [1887–1977], the wonderful singer Marian Anderson [1897–1993], and many, many others have proven that the path to the summit of art is in no way off-limits to the black race. In any case, the achievements of the mulattoes—the Negrid-European hybrids—are living proof against the doctrine of the harmfulness of miscegenation. Personalities such as the Negro leader Booker T. Washington [1856–1915], among others, must convince all who attempt to deny higher intelligence to the black race that this is not the case.[3] In spite of this, or perhaps because of it, in America the black race in itself is given little social value, and is being fought against on the political level. Here, we are for the first time encountering racism, the struggle against a group of people because of their race, with all its injustices and brutality—lynch mobs, etc. The following fact illuminates the true causes of the "racial hatred" of the Americans. While the "filthy" and "mean" American Indians were hated and despised as a race during the Yankees' conquest of North America, poetry and life later painted a saintly picture of the "brave" and "generous" Indians—indeed, today it is considered an honor in the truly hundred-percent Yankee families of the "Mayflower Americans" if a drop of Indian blood surfaces

---

3   See cover image of this book.

anywhere in the family tree, whereas mixing with Negro blood would be socially and politically impossible for those families. The explanation for this is clear. The race of the American Indians were only bad and contemptible when they were dangerous foes, when their land was being forcibly taken from them and their huts were being burned to the ground. Today, North America's Indians are dying out, their race is not dangerous—and therefore it is good. In contrast, the Negroes, whose numbers are growing quickly, and who with their modest lifestyles and skillfulness represent not entirely un-dangerous competitors, are "naturally" a bad race. However, the matter can take a different turn. There is also a question of the yellow race. The yellow, slant-eyed, "malicious" Japanese people are forbidden from immigrating to America and Australia, although the Chinese and Japanese have run out of space in their homelands— more so than the German "people without space." But when, in March 1933, "public rage" turned against all foreign races and thus against the Japanese who were living in Berlin, lo and behold!, a complaint by the Japanese embassy sufficed to have the official German channels confirm the goodness of the Japanese race and to strictly forbid all harassment. Why? Because Japan, as the greatest military power of the East, and indeed as a potential future ally of Germany, is extremely powerful. This is why the Japanese race is good. This minor observation that we have included in our scholarly presentation clearly demonstrates the significance of evaluating race—it exposes racism, whose existence and meaning we will consider later.

IV. The fourth large major race, the yellow or Mongolid, with its 600 million people, is, after the whites, the earth's largest and most powerful racial group. From their homeland, the Asian continent, they have spread even to America, where they mixed with Europid elements (in North America) and with Australid blood (in South America) to give rise to the various racial forms of the American Indians. They are also related to the Eskimos of the Arctic regions, who emerged out of the mixing of Mongolid forms with primeval, perhaps Ice-Age forms (Cro-Magnon or reindeer hunters). Mongols typically live in northern and southeastern Asia. They too demonstrate a clearly distinct race: light skin color with a yellowish base; thick skin with little beard growth; a mostly round or at best mid-length cranium; a flat face with strong cheekbones; a small, flat nose; eyes that appear squinty and slanted (the result of a peculiar development of the upper eyelids); firm black hair on the head—these are the most important features of the Mongolian race (Image 5), which according to Eickstedt should be subdivided into the western Sibirids, the northern Tungids, the eastern Sinids, and the southern Old-Mongoloids or Malayans. We find that all levels of culture are represented within the Mongolid major race, from the most primitive hunter and fisher cultures of the north (Gilyaks, Chukchis, etc.) to the ancient advanced civilizations of the Chinese and the powerful military culture of modern Japan. Even the most primitive Mongols cannot be described as being inferior. Anyone who has seen the image of the Eskimo mother radiating joy as she carries her child must also see the Madonna in her. And the pictures of leading Chinese and Japanese personalities (Image 6) demonstrate to every calm observer that the one human spirit bridges all differences of race.

V. While the four hitherto mentioned major races have been easy to characterize and categorize, a uniformly characterizing the largest major race, the Europid, is just as difficult as establishing clear divisions among the individual sub-races of which it is composed. In both number and power, this racial group outshines all others. Among the almost one billion people that are attributed to it, however, there are almost 400 million Indians and Near Easterners—i.e., scorned colors. Although there is no other place in the world that carries out more studies and measurements than here, distinguishing between racial types in the hodgepodge of Europe is much more difficult than anywhere else in the world. The vast majority of Europeans are diverse products of racial mixing, and contain numerous characteristics of other races in addition to those of their own, so that assigning them to one racial type or another seems difficult and virtually impossible without a large degree of arbitrariness. Furthermore, one should not forget that the so-called European races, which form the foundation for the distinctions and evaluation of new German racism, are closely related to one another. They are only sub-races of the one white Europid major race.

According to the older doctrine of three races elaborated by Ripley and others, the following distinctions are made within Europe: a blond, slender, tall, dolichocranial [long-skulled] type in the north, the Nordic or Germanic type; a brown, average-height, stocky, brachycranial [broad-skulled] type in central Europe, the so-called Alpine Race; and a dark-haired, short, dainty, dolichocranial type in the south, the so-called Mediterranean type. Later on, it was established that, in addition to the Alpine race, another race can be found in the Alps: although this one is also brachycranial, it is a tall and strong race with a large hooked nose and a steeply sloping occiput, and its people extend from here to the karst regions and on to southeastern Europe—it has been called the Dinaric race. Furthermore, another race has been established in eastern Europe in particular: although this race is brachycephalic and of medium height, it is ash blond and has light-colored eyes—it has been named the Ostic (East Baltic) racial type. In addition to these five races, however, various anthropologists have put forward a large number of further European racial types. The French researcher [Joseph] Deniker [1852–1918], one of the founders of modern race theory, divided the Mediterranean race into a southern branch, that of the Iberian Peninsula, and a western, Atlantic-Mediterranean branch: the former's smaller build and narrower skull is said to distinguish itself from the latter branch, which is of medium height and mesocephalic and which, according to Deniker, is related to the Cro-Magnon race of the Ice Age. The outstanding Polish anthropologist [Jan] Czekanowski [1882–1965] sorts out the European racial chaos by reducing it to four major races, which he designates the Nordic, the Mediterranean, the Lapponoid, and the Armenoid. He derives six further mixed races from these four major races. By mixing with the Armenoid race, the Lapponoid race from northern Europe produced the Alpine mixed race. Similarly, Czekanowski views the Dinaric race as a mixture of the Nordic and Armenoid races. Furthermore, he considers the ash-blond Ostic (East Baltic) race to be nothing other than a Nordic-Lapponoid mixed form. The Czekanowskian hypothesis, which emphasizes the close link between the Ostic racial type common in Poland and Russian and the Nordic race, has been disputed, however. It is just as likely that the Ostic type represents a blond form of an Asian race (blond Mongolids, according to [Gustav] Kraitschek [1880–1927]) that emerged through mutation or through the effects of the environment. Perhaps one of the subconscious motives that led to the elaboration of the hypothesis of the "sub-Nordic" Eastern race was that of national prestige. In the age of racism, kinship with the Nordic race is frequently emphasized—this kinship will, however, certainly be disputed by the German racists if politics requires it.

In recent years, attempts have been made to sketch out further Europid racial types. [Fritz] Paudler [*Die Hellfarbigen Rassen*, Prague, 1924] and others, for example, identified a race that is tall and blond like the Nordic race, but that is not slender but rather broad and "heavy," with a wide face (a "pentagonal face"); this race was named the Dalic type, and could represent a transitional race between the Nordic and the Ostic races. This type is said to be prevalent in certain parts of Sweden (Dalarna), but also in western Germany (Westphalia, which is why it is also called the "Phalian" race). Some have also attempted to trace this type back to the highest race of the Ice Age, the Cro-Magnon race, and have named it the Cro-Magnon race—although it is much more likely that the reindeer hunters of the Ice Age are closely related to the reindeer hunters of the present day, the Eskimos; all the more so since the two types of reindeer hunters are very similar not only in terms of their bodies but also in terms of their cultural contexts (Eskimo art). The new "Dalic racial type" was put forward when it was established that outstanding representatives of the German people (Otto von Bismark [1871–1890] and Paul von Hindenburg [1847–1934], among others) did not correspond to the ideal Nordic race. The Dalic race was thus also named the "Hindenburg race." There is no question that such an approach could also lead to the identification of several more characteristic races within the European population. For example, in his *Race Theory* [*Rassenkunde*], which is as fantastical as it is original, [Karl Felix] Wolff [1879–1966] establishes the new "Ario-primitive" racial type. As starting points for his elaboration of this race, he takes the bearded faces of [Leo] Tolstoy (1828–1910] and Charles Darwin [1809–1882], with their bushy eyebrows, deeply set eyes, and broad noses, which remind one of the racial type of the Ainus. There is no doubt that we could put forward a Tolstoy race alongside a Hindenburg race, as well as a Mussolini race, a Lenin race, and a Clemenceau race. It is, however, extremely doubtful whether making new races from such types, in whose elaboration the style of beard, etc. plays a role, is correct. Perhaps this approach will lead to a science of European facial and character types, which might then provide some benefit to racial science. Furthermore, comprehensive examination of the racial image of the European population results in more frequently recurring types. Many of these have likely emerged due to the fact that after much instances of miscegenation, certain combinations of features or hereditary characteristics demonstrate a special mutual attraction. When the germ plasm that was actuated through crossbreeding finds its equilibrium, new fixed linkage groups emerge, new racial types. This is how races came into being in the past—and this is how they can still come into being today, especially when the new forms of equilibrium demonstrate greater adaptation to the natural and social environment than the old primary races.

Ergon von Eickstedt [1892–1965] provides the most modern classification of the Europid major race in his massive *Race Theory and Racial History of Humanity* (Stuttgart: Ferdinand Enke, 1933). He divides the Europids into nine sub-races and three special forms. He distinguishes the following: a) two blond (depigmented) northern races, the dolichocranial blond Nordic race and the brachycranial ash-blond Ostic race; b) four brachycephalic races from the so-called "brachycephalic belt," namely, the aforementioned Alpine race, the Dinarid race, followed by the Armenid race, which represents a special Near Eastern form of the Dinarid, and which is distinguished from the Dinarid race by its smaller and stockier build, and finally the new Tunarid race, which Eickstedt puts forward for the first time, and which is at home in both the Near East and the steppes of central Asia, but which I believe should actually be viewed as a Europid-Mongolid mixed form; c) finally, three dolichocranial dark-haired races, namely, the South-Europid Mediterranean race, the closely related Orientalid race, and the dark-skinned Indid race, which probably emerged from the mixing of the Orientalid race with Veddid elements. Eickstedt considers the following to be special forms of the Europid formal circle: the South-Indian Veddas, the northern Japanese Ainus, and the Polynesians, who have their homes in Hawaii and other islands of the South Seas, for example. However, it must be emphasized that these possible anatomical links are hypothetical, after all, and may only represent so-called convergence phenomena.

In the following, we will provide a brief characterization of the diffusion and the physical characteristics of the most important European racial types.

1. The Nordic race's closed-off region of dissemination is in the coastal countries of the North Sea and the Baltic Sea, especially in Scandinavia; however, this race also makes up a large part of the population in England and northern Germany. A large percentage of the populations of North America, Australia, and other Anglo-Saxon colonies also belong to it. It is tall (173 cm on average) and long-limbed, its skull is long and narrow, its occiput round and bulging, its face long and narrow, its nose long and prominent, its hair blond; its eyes are light-grey or blue, and its skin is light and thin, turning red when exposed to the sun. The so-called asthenic constitution type (long, slender, lanky) bears a certain similarity to the Nordic racial type. The Nordic race has doubtlessly given humanity many tall men and women (Images 7 and 8). Through the photographs with which he adorns his books, Hans Günther [1891–1968] falsely elevates the impression of the Nordic race's superiority by selecting extremely favorable photographic subjects.

2. The Mediterranean race is located primarily in the coastal countries of the Mediterranean Sea, in Spain, Portugal, southern Italy, and the eastern coast of the Balkan Peninsula. But it also has settled in large parts of north Africa and the Near East, particularly in mixtures with the closely related Orientalid race. Like the Nordic race, its skull is long and narrow, however its forehead is somewhat steeper and more rounded, and its nose is straight and short (Image 9). It is shorter than the Nordic race (161 cm) and its skeleton is smaller and more delicate, its hair is dark, as are its eyes, and its skin is brownish, becoming slightly darker when exposed to the sun. It is assumed that it is related to the Nordic race, from which it is distinguished on account of the richness of its pigment and its small build—which is possibly a result of crossbreeding with an extinct dwarf race (the Grimaldi race?)—just as it is assumed to be related to the Oriental race of the Near East. It is possible that out of an originally uniform dolichocranial Eurasian race, the culture—or domestication—and the north with its lack of light and its cold gave rise to the partially albinotic

northern race, the "Xanthochroi" race, whereas the dark "Melanochroi" races in the south were not subject to this alteration. Eugen Fischer [1874–1967] has proposed a similar hypothesis.

3. The third European race, the Alpine race, has its primary area of settlement in central Europe, namely, in southwest and central France, in the Alps, in south and central Germany, in the Sudetenland, in Poland, Hungary, etc. Its skull is short with a round occiput, its face is round, its nose broad and coarse, its hair and eyes brown, its build short and stocky. The resemblance that this racial type bears with the so-called "pyknic" constitution type is striking (Images 10 and 11). The doctrine of the link between the Alpine racial type with the Mongolid race, which many authors take as certain—Günther names the latter as the former's purported origin because of the East Balkan race—is pure speculation and can be proven neither anthropologically—the Mongolian spot and the Mongolian fold[4] are missing—nor historically. Such a link would have to, in any case, go all the way back to the Stone Age. The possibility of an inundation of Mongolian blood in those primeval times was indeed there. After the primeval era, in historical times, massive Mongolian raiding parties from the Asian continent did indeed descend on Europe often enough—Huns and Tartars, Avars, Magyars. But a "seeping in" of inner-Asian blood, which the racists are constantly writing about, is out of the question. Rather, murder and fire are the legacy of Mongolian conquerors, just as they are the legacy of Viking-Nordic conquerors. Similarly, Czekanowski's view, which considers the Alpine race to be a mixture of the northeast-European Lapponoid race with the Armenoid race, is mere speculation.

4. The Dinaric race inhabits the Alps together with the Alpine race; however, it also inhabits, on a large scale, the west coast of the Balkan peninsula, the lands of Croatia, Bosnia, Serbia, Albania. The Tyrolean peasants in Defregger's paintings are of the Dinaric racial type, as are the warring Montenegrins and Arnauts. Its skull has a characteristic form: it is extremely short, but has a large forehead,

---

4   Translator's note: Today, this is generally referred to as the "epicanthic fold."

and is characterized by an oblate occiput. Its nose is particularly large and very bent, and the height of its body is considerable (168 to 172 cm). It is quite strongly pigmented, its hair and eyes are dark, its skin too is often brownish, and there is strong hair growth (Images 13 and 14).

5. The vast majority of the Ostic race (which Günther calls the "East Baltic" race) resides in eastern Germany, Poland, the peripheral states[5], the Sudetenland, and large parts of Russia. It has many commonalities with the Alpine race and is similarly stocky and broadly built, its skull is round, if somewhat smaller than the Alpine skull, its face is somewhat higher and often has a broad brow with distinct frontal eminences, a strong lower jaw with a non-prominent chin, at times prominent cheekbones and a flat nasal root with a broad, sometimes slightly upturned nose (Image 12). Its hair is blond or ash blond, its eyes light blue or gray, and sometimes somewhat squinty. The great Austrian poet Marie von Ebner-Eschenbach [1830–1916] is clearly of the Ostic type. The face of the Ostic race is also the "Slavic face," the face of Czech and Russian peasants, of German proletarians as Käthe Kollwitz [1867–1945] draws them—but it is also the face of many Russian and Polish Jews. The facial structure, the strong cheekbones, the often squinty eyes, all of this reveals a certain inclination toward the Mongolian type, the blond hair and light-colored eyes however a relation to the Nordic type. Whether we are here dealing with an established crossbreeding of two types, or whether one should see in the Ostic person the "blond Mongolid" who emerged through a mutation, is difficult to determine. There are transitional phases between the Ostic race and the Nordic one, and the former is linked to the latter through blondness, but there are also transitional phases between the Ostic race and the Alpine and "Turanid" race, and the former resembles the latter in its physique and facial structure. Heads such as Gorky's, for example, demonstrate a close relationship to the Ostic race, whereas the Turanid-Mongolid strain is more strongly expressed in Lenin's cranial and facial structures.

In ten interesting papers, which were published under the joint title "The Races of Central Europe: The Results of Anthropological Research" (*Die Rassen*

---

5   Translator's note: This refers to the states on the Western periphery of Russia.

Zentraleuropas – Ergebnisse anthropologischer Forschung), edited by Professor [Jindřich] Matiegka [1862–1941] of Charles University in the "Prague Press" between November 1934 and January 1935, leading anthropologists of various nations reported on the racial classification of populations in individual European countries. In one of these papers, Professor [Viktor] Lebzelter [1889–1936], the director of the anthropological division of the Natural History Museum in Vienna, takes up the results of anthropological research with regard to the races of Austria. He primarily ascertains the following: "Our findings from Austria's race studies are still a long way off from being able to portray the population's history on a racial foundation with any clarity." All the same, some discoveries, e.g., those of [von Klein] Hadersdorf, show that the brunette "Atlanto-Mediterranean" race, which is today indigenous to southwestern Europe, was probably indigenous to Austria in the early Stone Age. Then, at the beginning of the Bronze Age, the "Dinaric" Bell-Beaker people came to the land. Later, the so-called "Unetice" people, who were probably Nordic, appeared. But Hainburg's discoveries at Thebes, which were made at the same time, provide knowledge about a shorter, brachycephalic population with Mongolid features.... Even this brief elaboration demonstrates that thousands of years ago almost the same diversity of racial types was indigenous to the region of Austria as it is today.

A study that [Viktor] Lebzelter [1889–1936] recently carried out on Viennese soldiers showed that 14 to 16% were the blond Nordic type; ca. 20% were the narrow-skulled and brunette "Atlanto-Mediterranean" race; ca. 15% belonged to the Ostic (East Baltic) racial type; about 20% revealed a tall, blonde yet noticeably brachycranial type—likely a blond Dinaric type!—which Lebzelter describes as "Noric" or "Celtic"; and ca. 10% belonged to a short, small, and brachycephalic type, which according to Lebzelter is of eastern origin and which he describes as the "Pontic" or "Kurgan race." According to Lebzelter, the Alpine element plays a much smaller role in Vienna than it does in the countryside. Similarly, the Dinaric element has a much weaker presence in Vienna than it does in Tirol and Salzburg. The racial mixture that Lebzelter, one of the foremost authorities on the race relations of Austria, describes is thus quite diverse. Lebzelter introduces new racial designations—for example, the "Noric" and the "Pontic"—, and almost all other collaborators of the series of papers do the same. Thus, in that series, Lebzelter, who also deals with the races of Romania, puts forward a "Dacian" type; [Božidar (Božo)] Škerlj [1904–1961], who writes on the races of Yugoslavia, speaks of a "Savid" regional type[6]; Czekanowski, in his account of the race relations of Poland, discusses that country's "Lapponid" element in detail; and Bartucz, who reports on Hungary, discusses that country's characteristic "Pannonid" racial element. The fact that the authors have to repeatedly put new racial types forward for every region of Europe only shows us that the hitherto prevalent racial classification cannot do justice to the complicated and diverse racial mixture. It is to be hoped that these papers, which were published in the "Prague Press," will be collected together and expanded upon for publication in book form. That work would best allow people to recognize the complexity of the racial mixture and the racial variety of all European people, as well as the impossibility and irrationality of endeavors to favor individual races or even to cultivate pure races. Another result of these papers, which convey the most modern state of anthropological research, is that while there are estimations about the distribution of individual racial types within individual peoples, no precise scientific data exists—because the overwhelmingly large number of different mixed types makes determining exact figures impossible.

Thus, the figures put forward by the well-known German racist Günther in his *Race Theory of the German People*[7] (15th edition, 1930, p. 295) concerning the racial composition of the German people should be approached with great caution. He asserts that in Germany the Nordic race "may" make up 50% of the blood, the Alpine (which Günther calls the Ostic) 20%, the Dinaric 15%, the Ostic (which Günther calls the East Baltic) 8%, and the Dalic and the Mediterranean each 2%. Such careless and in truth utterly worthless estimations then make up the foundation of racist argumentation. In contrast to this, the precise racial investigations of the different regions of Germany

---

6   Translator's note: I cannot find any English equivalent for the German word *Saviden*. It is a neologism in German that seems to have never caught on.

7   *Rassenkunde des deutschen Volkes.*

that were carried out within the framework of *German Race Theory*[8] (edited by Prof. Eugen Fischer, who is associated with the racists) paint a completely different picture. In the eight volumes of this massive scientific compilation, which was published before Hitler's coup, the racist doctrine that the editor Prof. Eugen Fischer adopted after the coup is brilliantly disproven. In Volume II, for example, [Karl] Saller [1902–1969] examines the race of the Keuper-Franconians, who live in the countryside between Nuremberg and Ingolstadt. According to Saller's figures, 28.1% of these most German of Germans belong to the Alpine race, 14.1% to the Dinaric, 33.4% to the East Baltic, and 12.3% to the Dalic rice, whereas pure Nordic types are relatively rare. Similarly, in Volume IV, "The Fehmarns," Saller determines that these inhabitants of the similarly named islands in the North Sea[9] are predominantly East Baltic. They therefore belong to a race that the "race researcher" Günther describes as a slave race. As a further result of the thorough and meticulous research that has been published in *German Race Theory*, it turns out that longer heads are almost completely absent in southern and central Germany. Thus, in Miesbach, for example, a typical Bavarian locale, only 0.4% of the people measured were dolichocephalic, as opposed to 91.4% who were brachycephalic, and 8.2% who were mesocephalic. Even in North Frisia, the "most Nordic" region of German, only 4.9% of the people observed were dolichocephalics, as opposed to 61.6% brachycephalics, and 8.2% mesocephalics. Concerning hair color, it was determined to be 71.2% brown-black and 28.8% blond in Miesbach (Bavaria), and 49.2% brown and 51.8% blond in North Frisia. Finally, in North Frisia, 3.9% of people were found to have brown eyes, 79.5% to have blue eyes, and 16.6% to have eyes of mixed colors; and in Miesbach 30.6% of the people were found to have brown eyes, 37% blue eyes, and 32.4% mixed. If one considers dolichocephaly to be an essential feature of the Nordic race—and this is the general view—then one comes to the conclusion that this race constitutes only a minor strain within the German people. This conclusion becomes all

---

8   *Deutsche Rassenkunde.*

9   Translator's note: There is actually only one island, and it is located in the Baltic Sea, not the North Sea.

the more evident when we consider that only those individuals who have all three racial features—long skulls, blond hair, and blue eyes, a combination that is obviously much rarer—can truly count as Nordic.

The European peoples in general, and the German people in particular, constitute a diverse hybrid mixture of the most varied races. Today, this fundamental truth is evident to every educated person. In the anthology *The Danger Racial Fanaticism and the Persecution of Jews Poses to Christianity* (Lucerne 1935)[10], the Bishop of Debrecen, Dr. Desider Bathazar, writes the following on page 26: "Race theory may very well be the favorite activity of zoologists and biologists who waste their time looking for worthless curiosities. The stubborn adherents of race theory might find themselves humbled, however, due to the proven insight that the principle of the purity of races belongs in the world of fairy tales—namely as a result of an unconstrained mixing that, as if caused by an earthquake, the peoples of different races have achieved through millennia of mass migrations, adventures, military victories and defeats, as well as all kinds of journeys and undertakings."

The truth that this educated layman expresses in these sentences has long since been confirmed by rigorous science. Eugen Fischer, today's leader of the racists, was once a highly regarded researcher. In his famous work *The Rehoboth Basters*, he investigated the variability of the hybrid population that emerged due to the crossbreeding of Dutch people and Hottentots—and came to the conclusion that the population of Germany is every bit as diverse as that hybrid population. On page 190 of that work, he writes: "In terms of variability, the hybrid group is extremely similar to our population from Baden. One is literally impelled to the conclusion that our central European population is also a fully corresponding hybrid mixture." We need to be clear about what this conclusion by E. Fischer means. It states that the population of southern Germany is so hybridized that it seems to be a mixed population of Hottentots and whites! The leader of the German racists says this. What does this conclusion mean with respect to the talk of "German blood" and that of the "purity of blood?" Racism is based on lies, the German racial laws are built on lies and distortion!

---

10 *Die Gefährdung des Christentums durch Rassenwahn und Judenverfolgung* (Lucerne, 1935).

In the preceding, we have provided an overview of the facts painstakingly compiled by the natural sciences regarding the major races of the human species and the sub-races of the Europid major strain. From an objective point of view, it is not possible to draw any political consequences concerning the value or non-value of different races from either these scientific or these cultural-historical factual materials. But in our agitated age, in this time of struggle and the rise of new classes as races, racial questions crave recognition and seek to arouse people's interest, and so it is that a "science" is emerging that seeks to secure the advantage for its own race. Objective, impartial science becomes rare and difficult when "ownership relations" are affected. *However, the fact that a science allows itself to be led by inclinations and disinclinations without any self-criticism rather than by sober and unbiased knowledge can ultimately only lead to deceptive and dangerous ideologies—the movement from objective race research to blind, fanatical racism provides a sad example of this* [italics added].

Around the middle of the previous century, the French Count [Joseph Arthur] Gobineau (1816–1882), who as an envoy in Persia, Rio de Janeiro, and Sweden had come to know foreign peoples and races, was the first to attempt to prove, in his fantastically stimulating work *An Essay on the Inequality of the Human Races*, that all progress, all genuine culture was thanks solely to the "Aryan" race, who laid down laws as the master and conqueror of the world. He thereby abandoned the foundation of objective representation free of hatred or favoritism and introduced the disastrous method of evaluating races. Of course, Gobineau, a northern Frenchman, sees the purest Aryans in northern France, his homeland, which was also the homeland of the rapacious Normans. According to Gobineau, the Germans are racially inferior, since the best of their blood was spilled in the Thirty Years' War and its Aryan portion was greatly diminished. Gobineau's ideas re-appeared in a new form in the writings of the German-Polish Friedrich Nietzsche. He proclaimed the often misunderstood ideal of the "blond beast," that "Nordic legend" that served as the foundation for the fantasies of subsequent pseudoscience.

The megalomania of the Wilhelmine Period of Germany, which sought to redeem the world with warships and machine guns, found a herald and prophet in the German-writing Englishman [Houston Stewart] Chamberlain

[1855–1927]. In his corpulent work *The Foundations of the 19ᵗʰ Century* [1899] [*Die Grundlagen des 19. Jahrhunderts*], which is riddled with quotations and overrun with unproven claims, he teaches that all culture is a consequence of the Germanic race. He sees the noblest blood of Germanness, however, in the Vikings, those blond pirates that descended on all of Europe with murder and fire from the 8th to 11th century. In order to prove that we owe all progress to the "Aryans," he designates all the great trailblazers of culture—Plato, Christ, Dante, Michelangelo, etc.—as Germanic people, without a moment's hesitation. Any thorough review will demonstrate the value of such claims. For example, [Giuseppe] Sergi [1841–1936] and [Fabio] Frasetto [1876–1953] have proven, in a scientifically sound study, that Dante—according to the information of his contemporaries, and to portraits of him from his lifetime, and primarily according to the skeleton that they investigated—belonged to the Mediterranean race that inhabits Italy to this day. But Chamberlain conferred the "Aryan degree" not only on prominent individuals, but also on entire peoples—on the French, Italians, Russians, etc., whose cultural significance he cannot deny. Chamberlain's *Foundations* had a massive influence on pre-war Germany. It was a favorite book of Kaiser Wilhelm II, who gave lavishly bound copies away to his friends. The boundless adulation of one's own race—which every educated person should view as being just as tasteless as self-praise—evoked, among large sections of the German aristocracy and bourgeoisie, an exaggerated faith in the "German mission" and the "German essence that shall cure the world," and also evoked dangerous underestimations of other peoples, a state of mind that future historians would consider one of the partial causes of the World War. The further elaboration of racism, the doctrine that race is the motor of history, that there are only a few noble and aristocratic races, or just one such race, to which human culture owes its existence and which therefore deserves to lead that culture—this is largely the work of Count [Georges de] Lapouge [1854–1936] in France and of [Ludwig] Woltmann [1871–1907] and [Ludwig] Gumplowicz [1838–1909] in Germany.

In the World War, Aryans fought against Aryans, and the Germanic Englishmen named the Germanic Germans "Huns," who returned the favor with their slogan "May God punish England"—on no account did blood prove "thicker" than water. But despite all this, or perhaps precisely because of it, racism rose up in Germany, borne by the passions of the post-war period, to ever-greater heights. The nation was defeated in the war, and the bourgeois class was driven back by the "revolution" of 1918, at least for a while. Germany's bourgeoisie, its youth, and its science inevitably sought out compensation vis-à-vis the hard facts, and through "masculine protest," at least in their imaginations. A whole host of young researchers endeavored to establish, by means of the past, the supremacy of the Germanic people, which the present was calling into question. If works such as those by Gobineau, Chamberlain, and others had previously been granted a place in "belles lettres," very similar currents were now becoming apparent in official German research. In the science of the inheritance of human traits, it was first the hypotheses of the zoologist August Weismann, and then the research of the Augustinian friar from Brno, Gregor Mendel [1822–1884], that laid the foundation for a theory that asserted the immutability of hereditary factors, their inability to be altered by external conditions. Mendelism was used to support the view that there are, by nature, higher and lower races, and that these differences are hereditary, or rather that they are permanently fixed. Lamarckism, which seeks to prove the emergence of new races through the influence of the environment, was rejected and fought against as a "Jewish" phenomenon. Reputed geneticists, anthropologists, and prehistorians are promoting the ideas of the Germanic racial aristocracy.

There is no question that racist propaganda literature has paved the way for the "national uprising." First, the journalist and literary figure Otto Hauser [1874–1932] emerged as a prophet of racism, though the public rated his numerous books on race merely as questionable journalistic and political achievements. Then, however, came the race messiah himself. [Hans Friedrich Karl] Günther [1891–1968], a former high school teacher, is the author of the racist community's "holy books." His *Race Theory of the German People* [*Rassenkunde des deutshen Volkes*, 1922] has gone through numerous print runs in the span of a few years. That work and Günther's other racial picture books, which the Lehmann press in Munich, in a favorable economic situation, repeatedly published, have become the gospel of the "educated" German youth and have profoundly influenced their mentality. Whoever has read Günther is ripe for the reading of *Mein Kampf*!

Günther has a very skillful method of racist propaganda. From somewhat arbitrarily chosen photographs, he constructs not only the races but also the different racial strains. As examples for the "agreeable" races, and particularly for the Nordic race, he selects beautiful heads with elegantly done hair from the upper classes of society; for the "disagreeable" races, e.g., the Alpine or Jewish races, the selection is less favorable. His peculiar style is then added to this, whereby some subjective opinion or other is introduced with a "perhaps" or "probably," only for him to cite this opinion, which was initially expressed in passing, as a fact a few lines later, and to draw all the conclusions that follow from it. Max Brod [1884–1968], in his small book *Race Theory and Judaism* (1935),[11] aptly characterizes this "maybe-science": "If Günther were to assess his work in his own style, he 'might' 'perhaps' say: In these books, the presumed amount of unproven sentences—as opposed to those that can, in many cases, be proven—can probably be estimated at a variable 23%, and the unproven underlying figures at roughly somewhere in the region of two thirds." Anyone who has read Günther's books will recognize his syle in this both successful and humorous caricature. Of course, the fact that the German Aryan legislation was built on such a maybe-science is much less humorous.

Günther's books provide few new facts. Günther adopts the race-related elements that were established by the research in Europe and that have also been proven in Germany. He has invented new, but in no way felicitous, names for them. He thus, without sufficient reason, designates the Mediterranean race as the "Westic" race; and he names the Alpine race—using its name to assert its very hypothetical origin—the "Ostic" race, and must therefore invent the new designation "East Baltic" for Deniker's Ostic race. Günther determines that six major races—according to his nomenclature, the Nordic, the Phalian (or Dalic), the East Baltic, the Ostic, the Dinaric, and the Westic—and five minor races, namely the Near Eastern, the Oriental, the Hamitic, the Negric, and the Mongolian strains, play a role in the composition of the German people. Not

---

11 Max Brod, *Rassentheorie und Judentum* (Barissia, 1934; Wein: R. Löwit, 1936).

only does Günther know, as the common person does, that physical racial qualities must somehow be connected to intellectual life, he also knows quite precisely which intellectual qualities, what cultural significance, and which cultural achievements are characteristic of each of the many races. He thus cleanly analyzes the German racial chaos with its eleven elements, precisely determines the distribution of those elements, and then hands out—he was a high school teacher, after all—report cards with grades ranging from "excellent" to "inadequate" to each individual racial component at his own discretion.

The Nordic race, of course, receives a grade of "excellent." It is not only the most beautiful but also the most noble, the master race of the world: "the Nordic man is the most militarily inclined." The fact that the pirates and robber barrons do not exactly appeal to the democrats and proponents of peace hardly bothers Herr Günther, for he hates democracy and despises the pacifists—and in this way as well he is a trailblazer for the morals of the Third Reich. The Ostic race, which science calls the Alpine, is, on the other hand, classified as "inadequate." This is not only the race that forms the greater part of the population in Switzerland, central France, and Czechoslovakia; it is also the race that is predominant in central and southern Germany. It is the race of [Ludwig van] Beethoven [1770–1827] and [Franz] Schubert [1797–1828], of Jean Paul [1763–1825] , and also of Gregor Mendel, whose work laid the foundation for all modern race theory. Herr Günther says, however, that the Ostic race has "seeped in from Asia"—he says that the Ostic soul is surly, slow, and petty, that it lacks all exuberance, that the "petit-bourgeois spirit" of the Ostic race corresponds to the sovereign spirit of the Nordic race, that Ostic girls are clumsy and lacking in grace (Image 11), etc. Herr Günther "says so—and is an honorable man." The other races come out a bit better. But only the noble Nordic race is culturally creative. Wherever Nordic blood runs dry, great cultures fall into ruin, and the most powerful empires perish. The blood of the Alpine, the "Ostic" race, however, is like a plague that has seeped into Europe from Asia, and that has brought democracy—that pestilence, that evil Asian legacy—upon the Nordic people. Half of Germany has already been "easternized"—Günther sees salvation only in the Nordic Internationale. Germanic peoples of all lands, unite! Blonde men, reproduce! Blonde women, bear children! Or the world will sink helplessly in the Alpine flood!

In the decade from 1920 to 1930, the Lehmann publishing house in Munich, the bookselling arsenal of German racism, produced, in truly rabbit-like fashion, more and more new books on race in the Güntherian direction—the success was the reward for bookselling acumen! Tens of thousands of books were sold, they were read, recommended in the national press, and enthusiastically discussed in numerous talks. That is how that attitude arose that glorifies one's own race while scorning the foreign race, an attitude which, as a matter of course, avails itself of the brutal repression of all who are different or alien as a right of the master race, the master *Volk*.

Official German science demonstrated benevolent neutrality towards pseudoscientific racism. Indeed, renowned scholars such as Eugen Fischer [1874–1967], Fritz Lenz [1887–1976], [Gustaf] Kossinna [1858–1931], [Ludwig] Wilser [1850–1923], and others publicly promoted the racial hype, and supported the new direction by cooperating with racist authors and by training young people in the racist thought process. Even in the big, otherwise scientifically valuable textbooks and handbooks, e.g., in the well-known *Sketch of the Doctrine of Human Heredity and Racial Hygiene* (*Grundriß der menschlichen Erblichkeitslehre und Rassenhygiene* [1921]) by Baur, Fischer, and Lenz, and in [Walter] Scheidt's *Race Theory* (*Rassenkunde* [1925])—both of which were published by the Lehmann house!—there is a lack of the objectivity that is to be expected from books that are exposed to the criticism of international science. In the illustrated monthly journal *People and Race* (*Volk und Rasse*), which was also published by Lehmann, the Güntherian trend found a kind of central mouthpiece. In the *Journal for Racial Physiology* (*Zeitschrift für Rassenphysiologie*) published by the Reche press, the attempt—which the findings of research into blood groups has shown to be futile—was even made to distinguish human races by their blood and thereby give the "myth of blood" a real foundation.

Within German science, almost no objection was raised against the nonsense of racism. Almost no one was there who would point to the fact that the value judgments by which the individual closely-related European races were weighed against one another were purely subjective and have precious little to do with science. It is quite a wonder that Herr Günther did not long ago receive the fitting reply to his outrageous claim about the "positional distinctions of the Germans according to their blood" from the "inferior" Alpine or Ostic Germans. A lone courageous fighter finally emerged from the University of Kiel, the lecturer Dr. [Friedrich] Fritz Merkenschlager [1892–1968], a thoroughly German and indeed nationalistic scholar, who in his splendid small book *Gods, Heroes, and Günther: a Repudiation of Güntherian Race Theory* (*Götter, Helden und Günther – eine Abwehr der Günther'schen Rassenkunde* [Nürnberg, 1927]) raised his voice against the irruptive intellectual epidemic. "I accuse this book of a crime against the intellectual life of the German people," Merkenschlager writes, who sees the crime of the Güntherian book in "that it strives to put millions of good and excellent Germans into the dungeon of inferior race and cut them off from the light." This small book, a futile warning at the last hour, concluded with a call: "Enough! Calls of 'Enough!' must ring out from every group of German compatriots as soon as the word 'race' is used in any sense other than the modest one."

Merkenschlager's warning was no use. Racism as a theory continued to feed hungrily, like an insidious fever—until all of a sudden the illness became acute, and the swelling bulge of practical, political racism burst open. The events in Germany have shown the world what a dangerous poison racism is for the nation or people infected by it. Racism should be considered a contagious disease in the present time of enormous crisis, in this time of fierce struggle for the existence of individuals and peoples, and one should immunize oneself against it as against a contagious disease before it is too late!

German political racism, which has become the "heart" of the National Socialist worldview, a "Nazi Ark of the Covenant" (P. Cyrill Fischer [Austrian priest and resistance fighter 1892–1945]), is based on the slogan of the supremacy of the "Aryan race." The concept "Aryan" or "Indo-Germanic" was coined by linguistic researchers who identified the connection of the Indian Sanskrit language with certain Near Eastern languages (Persian, Armenian, etc.) on the one hand, and with the European, or rather Germanic, languages on the other. They assumed that Sanskrit had been brought with the conquerors that had penetrated India from the north, and who called themselves "Aryas," which denotes "the fair ones." But there is no indication that these conquerors were Germanic, or even that they belonged to the Nordic race. In a recent paper, the Indian [sociologist] Bhupendranath Datta [1880–1961] determines that four racial types, or rather biotypes, can be distinguished among the northern Indian population, and goes on to write: "Concerning the widespread view that the first biotype is linked to the blond, dolichocranial element of northern Europe, it has been determined that neither the Vedas nor Sanskrit literature make mention of a blond racial type, and that the theory of the influx of this racial type from the north into this region cannot be proven from the perspective of Mendelism and the science of hybridity."[12] As is well known, the strict separation of castes exists in India to this day, which forbids all mixing of the privileged upper castes with the lower ones—an ideal institution from the standpoint of racism, since it best guarantees the purity of the race. However, this racism, which has been practically applied for a thousand years, has brought no luck to the Indian people—today, there is hardly a more physically miserable and wretched people on the face of the earth. If we examine the Indian upper castes anthropologically, we find neither a trace of blondness nor any other features of the Nordic race—which in the caste system should have been preserved precisely in the upper castes, who are descendants of the conquerors. In contrast, every photograph of a gathering of rajas and maharajas reveals the typical image of the Oriental race in the vast majority of these most authentic of "Aryas"! (Image 28). The Aryan conquerors could rightly call themselves the "Aryas," the "fair ones," for they were much fairer than the dark-skinned, dark-brown to brown-black Gondid and Veddid native population. But like the other inhabitants of the Near East, they were Orientals—perhaps with a stronger admixture of Armenid and Turanid elements, and a weaker admixture of blond elements, as we still find among certain peoples of the Near East today, e.g., the Kurds. The fact that these Orientals spoke a non-Semitic language changes nothing about their

---

12 Bhupendranath Datta, "Eine Untersuchung über die Rassenelemente in Belutschistan, Afghanistan und den Nachbarstaaten des Hindukusch" ["An Investigation into the Racial Elements in Balochistan, Afghanistan, and the Neighboring States of the Hindu Kush"], Charlottenburg 1923. [*Hugo Iltis' note*]

racial affiliation. There is no stable relationship between race and language. There are Germans from the Alpine, Dinaric, and Nordic races. The Ostic race includes many Hungarians, who speak a Finno-Ugric language, as well as many Poles, who speak an Indo-Germanic language. The old Indian Aryan fable that assumed a racial link between the Sankrit people and the Nordic race, falls to pieces when exposed to critical review! A relationship between the genuine Indian "Aryans" and the Jews is much more likely, as the Oriental racial element plays a significant role in both of them. The Indian conquerors, the true Aryans, were Orientals—it is important to explicitly emphasize this point!

Apart from this, the concept "Aryan" was also introduced to designate a language community. Scientists have repeatedly stressed that although one can speak of Aryan languages, there is no Aryan race. Even the racist themselves, such as Chamberlain, Günther, and others, have given up using the designation "Aryan race" and instead only speak of a Germanic, or rather Nordic, race. But the racist politicians of the Third Reich are not concerned with the scruples of their own prophets, and continue to preach the "Aryan racial ideal," to publish "Aryan articles," and to demand that civil servants, medical doctors, etc. be of "Aryan descent." Dr. [Johann] von Leehrs [1902–1965], who wrote the notorious inflammatory tract "Jews are looking at you" ("Juden sehen Dich an"), cynically admits that scientific motivations no longer matter in Germany: "The word Aryan," he writes, "is primarily a word to repel Jews and culturally uncreative races!"

Thus: The word Aryan has absolutely no scientific or rational significance. The German people are in no way composed of a single race, but rather of at least eleven different races that are no less distinguishable from one another than the racial elements of the Jewish group—and yet the one group are summarized as inferior non-Aryans while the other group are called noble Aryans, so that the former can be fought against and persecuted by the latter! "They want to exterminate the Jews like snakes or predators, and to this end they must naturally first turn them into snakes or predators" (Theodor Lessing [German Jewish philosopher, 1872–1933]). Such a mentality, which rejects reason as an argument and only accepts violence as valid, obviously entails, in terms of its consequences, the end of Western civilization!

We have Felix von Luschan [1854–1924] to thank for the first thorough scientific examinations of the race of the Jews. He strove to unravel the racial chaos of the Near East, the original Jewish homeland, and managed to solve that region's racial riddle. Among all the peoples that inhabit the Near East, the Armenians—some of whom formed a self-contained settlement in the mountainous region of the Wannsee, and a total of four million of whom are also scattered around the world—most purely embody the race of the original native population. They are a dark-skinned breed of medium height with a pronounced round skull whose distinguishing features are a steep oblate occiput and a strongly hooked nose (Images 15 and 16). This race has lived in the Near East for many thousands of years, it was the race of the ancient Hittites, which already had an advanced civilization in the second millennium BC, and which were not confined to backwater areas as today's Armenians are, but rather were scattered across the entire Near East. One can see that the Hittite and the Armenian are the same racial type from the preserved stone reliefs of their kings and gods. The famous inscription from Sendschirli,[13] which [Felix von] Luschan [1854–1924] excavated in 1888, proves that these Hittites possessed a written language, from which the Phoenician and Greek alphabets, as well as all subsequent alphabets, could be derived. According to research by the famous Czech scholar Friedrich Hrozny [1889–1952], the language of these inscriptions was an Indo-European one. We can see from this conclusion that the bearer of one of the first Indo-European, or rather "Aryan," cultures was a people that was racially much closer to the Jews than to the blond Nordic race. It is very probable that the founders of the Indo-European language and cultures have nothing in common with present-day blond Germanic people. The Hittite racial type lives on in present-day Armenians and is therefore called the "Armenoid" by Luschan. Eugen Fischer names it the "Near Eastern" racial type (Images 15 and 16). A comparison of racial descriptions reveals a pronounced similarity with the Dinaric race of Europe and Germany, which, moving from the Alps over the karst regions to the Balkans and on to the Near East, finds

---

13 Translator's note: This is now more commonly known as Sam'al, a kingdom in the Middle East that existed between 1725 BC and 1200 BC.

its geographic continuation in the Near Eastern race (Image 13 and 14). Eugen Fischer writes the following about the Near Eastern race: "it is extraordinarily close to the Dinaric race described above, only its small height distinguishes it. The two could be sister races."

The second racial element that already played a role in the Near East several thousand years before Christ is the Oriental race, which was probably brought to the Near East by Semitic peoples from their original Arabian homeland. According to Luschan, today this racial type only remains pure in the mountainous interior of Arabia: it exhibits fair skin, i.e., no darker than the southern Europeans, dark, soft, curly hair, and slender skulls with elongated faces and small, slender noses that are sometimes straight and sometimes hooked. Eugen Fischer writes the following about this race: "The Oriental race may be very close to the Mediterranean race—two branches from a single root." Most present-day Arabs, which make up a large part of the population of Syria and Palestine, reveal this Oriental racial type—not purely, of course, but rather strongly mixed with the more ungainly Near Eastern race.

The third racial component that Luschan pulls out of the Near Eastern mix comes, in his view, from the blond-haired Nordic strains. Scythians, Iranians, and other peoples with a Nordic admixture are said to have borne this Nordic element to the Near East and Palestine, where it is said to have played a significant role among the Amorites, the Philistines, and others.

This blond Nordic element has also been preserved within a Near Eastern strain of people, namely: the marauding Kurds, whose center of distribution lies in Kurdistan, a mountainous country in southern Armenia. From a sample of 221 Kurds, Luschan found that 53% were blond and blue-eyed.

"All the large groupings of peoples that we find in the Near East today," Luschan writes, "are made up of these three elements: the Armenoids, the Semites, and the northern Europeans." With his thorough studies of the Near East, Luschan also sheds light on the problem of the racial affiliation of the Jews. Even the Palestinian Jews of ancient times were no pure race, but rather represented a mixed people, a so-called population, in which the Near Eastern, the Oriental, and the Nordic racial elements played the major roles (Image 22). The skull measurements that Luschan carried out on 1222 Near Eastern Jews demonstrated that the modern Jews are a similarly mixed population and in no way a pure race. The result of these measurements was depicted in a curve with two clear peaks. Among the people examined, there was a clearly prominent group with narrow heads—with a cephalic index of circa 75—and a second very distinct group with round heads. It is primarily the Armenoid element (and perhaps also a Turanid admixture) that lies in the mendelized round heads; and it is primarily the Oriental, or rather Mediterranean, element—and perhaps also the Nordic strain—that lies in the long heads.

Later on, this Luschanian doctrine—which, by the way, was also adopted by Chamberlain and Günther, albeit with a tendentious attitude—was expanded and made more complete. It is in any case certain that the Jews, whether one considers them as a people or merely as a community that fate has thrown together, do not represent a race, but rather a mixed-race population, just like all the other modern European peoples. The hypothesis of [Ignaz] Zollschan [1877–1944], who speaks of a uniform Jewish type, is based solely on the fact that the thousand-year-old, uniform, urban, commercial, and intellectual environment produced a certain unity of affectation, speech, and facial expressions. In the Middle Ages and the early modern period, the Jews were not only a religious community but also a caste, a social class unto themselves. But this uniform "Jewish type" that the environment generated in a relatively short period of time—for even a millennium is a short time when it comes to lasting biological change—is only a modification, and could be modified again by a different environment, e.g., through assimilation or through normal occupational structures within the Jewish group, as the settlements in Palestine or in Birobidzhan will entail. This "uniform" Jewish type has nothing to do with with race in the biological sense—the Jews are and will remain a mixed-race population!

Many aspects of the racial composition of today's Jewish population can be explained historically. After the Babylonian exile and especially after the Romans' destruction of Jerusalem, there was a mass migration of Jews to places throughout the civilized world—the Diaspora.

Two main currents led to the formation of two physically and also culturally distinct Jewish types. Those Jews who came to Eastern Europe from the Near

East through the Caucasus and the Black Sea constitute the groups of Eastern Jews or Ashkenazim; the others, who spread out along the coasts of the Mediterranean, constitute the Southern Jews or Sephardim, and they settled in Spain in particular during the period of Moorish rule. Both types have much in common, and in no way do they stand in stark contrast to one another. But it is also not acceptable to deny their differences, as many authors, including Zollschan, do.

Among the Spaniolic Jews, who today represent the Sephardic element, the daintier Oriental type and the related Mediterranean type are more prominent. The Armenoid, Turanid, and Nordic elements play a smaller role with them. They are small and dainty, mostly with dark brown hair and narrow heads and faces; their women occasionally display the noble beauty of the southerners. Today's Spaniolic Jews are the descendants of the Jews who were driven out of Spain in 1492 and out of Portugal in 1496, some of whom settled in the north (England and Holland), but most of whom settled in Turkey and the Levant (Salonica, etc.). In Germany, the Spanish strain can be found particularly among the Jews on the Rhine.

The much larger portion of today's Jews, namely the Jews of Russia and Poland, but also those of America—most of whom originally came from Eastern Europe—belong to the Eastern Jewish or Ashkenazi group. The Oriental-Mediterranean element recedes into the background among these Jews. In contrast, the Armenoid racial element, which is related to the Dinaric, plays a significant role. However, new studies—in particular the work of [Maurice] Fischberg [1872–1934], [Samuel] Weißenberg [1867–1928], Eugen Fischer [1874–1967], [Ignacy Maurycy] Judt [1875–1923], [*Die Juden als Rasse* (The Jews as a Race), Berlin, 1903], [Jan] Czekanowski [1882–1965], G. Lempert, [Salomon] Czortkower [1903–1943], [Jindřich] Matiegka [1862–1941, *The Equality of European Races*, 1933], and others—have shown that the other racial elements of the European population, among whom the Jews have been living for over a thousand years, also play a role. The main types of the Russian and Polish populations can be found among them, namely the dark, brachycephalic Alpine (or Lapponoid, according to Czekanowski) racial type, and the ash-blond, brachycephalic Ostic (sub-Nordic, according to Czekanowski) racial type; as well as the Oriental-Mediterranean and the Nordic types, albeit to a lesser degree. [Rudolf] Virchow's [1821–1902] anthropology of schoolchildren (1874–77) has shown the extent to which the blond element has spread among the Jews of Eastern and Central Europe: he determines that among German-Jewish schoolchildren, 11% have fair skin, blond hair, and blue eyes; 42% have dark skin, brown and black hair, and dark eyes; while the remaining 47% are composed of mixed forms between the fair and dark types. The percentage of blondness among Russian Jews is higher still. It is difficult to determine whether this blondness is to be explained through the groupings of characteristics from those supposed ancient miscegenations in the Near Eastern homeland—with the Amorites, Philistines, etc.—or through later miscegenations with Nordic or Ostic elements, or whether mutations caused the sudden emergence of blond types among the Jewish population. Among the other characteristics of the Jewish population, it should be mentioned that the skull is often mesocephalic—but dolichocephalics are also present, particularly among the Spaniolic Jews. The average head size of Eastern Jews is 163 cm. In Rhodes, however, where they have a monopoly on the porter business, among the 67 Jews that Luschan measured, 11 had heads over 180 cm long, and the average size was 174 cm—they were thus real giants. Zollschan, incidentally, made similar observations in Salonica.

Detailed historical studies will, in the future, have to demonstrate how racial elements from the European population that surrounded them were absorbed, despite their religious uniformity. The miscegenations in question likely took place in the early Middle Ages. Today, in any case, the European Jews offer an image of an extremely mixed popluation in which the same racial elements that play a role in the rest of the European population are present—albeit in slightly different proportions. Images 24 to 27 show four heads of prominent Jewish scholars—and simultaneously four clearly recognizable racial types. The Southern Jews show a close racial relationship to the peoples of southern Europe, among whom the Jews are physiognomically relatively inconspicuous. The Eastern Jews show the same racial elements as the peoples of eastern Europe. The Near Eastern element that emerges more strongly among the Eastern Jews occasionally brings about a striking similarity to certain types among the Dinaric peasants from the Alps—a similarity that often has a comic effect, since the environmental features of the two types are diametrically opposed. The proportions in which the individual racial elements appear among the Jews are, of course, not easy to determine in terms of numbers or percentages, just as any such data must be viewed with great caution. According to studies by G. Lempert on Jewish university students in Lemberg, circa 16.7% represent the Nordic, or rather sub-Nordic, type, 2.7% the East Baltic, 14.7% the Alpine, 12% the Lapponoid, 2.7% the Dinaric, 9.3% the Armenoid, 12% the Mediterranean, and 18.7% the Oriental type. According to data from Czortkower, the Jews of Central Europe reveal circa 21.5% Nordic race, 23.8% Lapponoid, 20.3% Armenoid, 18.4% Mediterranean, and 15.9% Oriental. However, it must once again be stressed that such seemingly precise statistics are to be treated with great caution in view of the very inexact research methods and the large jumble of research material. Only one thing can be derived with any certainy from all this data: that in the diverse racial mixture that the Jewish population represents, all elements belong to the Europid major strain. The Jews therefore in no way represent a foreign or Asian race!

One can no more speak of a uniform or homogeneous mixed race with regard to the Jews as one can with regard to any other European people. Such a concept of a uniform mixed race contradicts our biological views, which were established by Mendelism. It must repeatedly be stressed that the Jewish type that is uniform in certain respects is only a result of the earlier ghetto environment, which was homogeneous to all Jews—it will disappear when the environments of the Jews become just as diverse as they are with other peoples.

Examining the portraits of prominent Jewish personalities allows us to see that the Jews belong to the various types of the European racial sphere. An interesting photograph shows us, for example, the Jewish painter [Max] Liebermann [1847–1935] in front of the portrait of [Paul] Hindenburg that he painted (Image 21). We can clearly see two racial types: the heavy blond type of the General beside the slender dark-haired type of the painter. But we can also clearly see that they are both European types—the type of the doyen of German painting could just as well be the type of an Italian or French statesman.

We have shown that the racial analysis of European Jews identified the same or virtually the same racial elements as are present in the other parts of the European population. It has been proven that there are millions of German

"Aryans" whose ethnicity cannot be contested by anyone and yet who, in their Alpine-Dinaric mixture, are farther removed from the purely Nordic ideal racial type than many thousands of their German-Jewish compatriots who in racial terms are frequently Mediterranean-Nordic (Images 20 and 26). Race therefore provides—and this cannot be demonstrated often enough—no grounds to make a distinction between Germans and German Jews or even to exclude the Jews as "foreign-blooded" from the German people.

The Jews are no foreign race. But might they perhaps be a foreign people that cannot and should not mix with the other European peoples? Under the term "people" [*Volk*], we understand a community of persons who seem to be connected to one another through a common language and culture, a common homeland and destiny. The German Jews were certainly not a normal community of people. A common language was lacking; and as the religion that had earlier produced a kind of cultural bonding gradually lost its significance, a common culture was also lacking. In the past, the German Jews were indeed a community of common destiny, unified through hardship and persecution. But ever since Germany—at least in theory—granted them equal rights, they bound their fate with that of Germany, felt themselves to be German, lived and worked for a German fatherland.

But the rift that had been closed was repeatedly torn open again—reference to the Eastern Jews, who have yet to be assimilated in their clothing and lifestyle, suffices to show this. The description that Hitler provides in *Mein Kampf* of the moment that actually turned him into an anti-Semite is typical. It was in Vienna, the "Babylon of races": "One day when I was walking through the inner city," we read on page 59/73,[14] "I suddenly came upon a being clad in a long caftan, with black curls. Is this also a Jew? was my first thought. At

---

14 Translator's note: For all quotations from *Mein Kampf,* unless otherwise noted, I am using the English version produced by John Chamberlain et al.: *Mein Kampf: Complete and Unabridged.* Editorial sponsors: John Chamberlain, et al. Reynal & Hitchcock, New York 1941. It is available online at: https://archive.org/stream/meinkampf035176mbp/meinkampf035176mbp_djvu.txt.
The page numbers given throughout refer first to the German original that Iltis cites, and then to the English version (i.e., German/English). I have occasionally modified the translation very slightly to bring it closer to the original German.

Linz they certainly did not look like that. Secretly and cautiously I watched the man, but the longer I stared at this strange face and examined one feature after another, the more my mind reshaped the first question into another form: Is this also a German?"

The sight of a Polish Jew, who would certainly never have thought to call himself a German, was enough to make the millions of German Jews seem like a "foreign people" in Hitler's eyes, and to allow to sprout up within him that attitude that would, twenty years later, find its violent expression in the German race laws.

In the writings and speeches of the Führer and his Youth, "the Jew" is described as Satan and criminal, as the malicious originator of all the German people's suffering. He is to blame for Germany losing the war—for Jewish Marxism robbed the fighting German army of victory by "stabbing it in the back." And he is also to blame for the fact that Germany has yet to win any new war—for Jewish pacifism negotiated with the enemy instead of striking them. The Jew must be annihilated—Hitler clothes this in the respectable formula *Juda verrecke!* ["Death to the Jews!"]—and then German will rise to its former greatness.

The psychological roots of the Hitler-people's hatred of the Jews lies first of all in the intellectual origins of Hitler's program within the program of [Georg Ritter von] Schönerer [1842–1941] and the German-Austrian students, whose "Waidhofen principle" [that Jews are not capable of understanding the German's idea of honor"] already, 30 years ago, denied the Jews the right to demand satisfaction in duels; and secondly in the hatred of unemployed intellectuals and ruined petit bourgeois against their disagreeable Jewish competitors; and finally, thirdly, in the despair that emerges from the awful economic conditions in postwar Germany and that seeks, by turning the defenseless Jews into scapegoats, to vent itself in the direction of the slightest resistance.

And yet how unjust and base this smear campaign against the German Jews is! They have resided in Germany for 1000 years. When the fortifications of Cologne had to be torn down after the war, an ancient Jewish cemetery was found that dated back to the time of Colonia Agrippina, the Roman city.

A similar cemetery is located near Mainz. Gravestones over a thousand years old stand in the Jewish cemetery in Worms. Such ancient Jewish cemeteries can be found from the lowland of the Rhein to Rothenburg ob der Tauber.[15] Free Jews were in the service of Carl the Great [Charlemagne, 742–814 C.E.]. It was the fanaticism of the Crusades that first brought the Jews into the ghetto. The Jews have a greater right to consider Germany their home than millions of present-day Germans, in particular today's Prussians, who just a few hundred years ago were Germanized Slavs! For centuries the forefathers of Hitler have been locking up German Jews in urban ghettos, letting their bodies and minds waste away; for centuries the Jews have been kept away from arable land and farming work, just as they have been kept out of civil and military service; for centuries trade and finance have been the only sources of livelihood made available to them—so isn't it natural that both the good and bad qualities of city dwellers and merchants have developed particularly strongly in them? It is because of the environment, and not because of race or "blood," that the German Jews have become what they are.

The ghetto walls first fell for some of the Jews after the French Revolution, about 100 years ago, and then for all of the Jews in 1848, and the emancipation had begun. And what have the tiny group of German Jews accomplished since they were granted human rights, since Lessing showed the German people the path of humaneness in *Nathan the Wise*? How these few hundred thousand people have worked for German art and science, for German culture, how they've struggled and wrestled for the greatness of the German name! Who can imagine German poetry without Heinrich Heine's [1797–1856] *Book of Songs* [1827], or German music without Felix Mendelssohn's [1809–1847] compositions? When German male choral societies sing the beautiful song *Wer hat dich, du schöner Wald?* ["Who Made You, Beautiful Forest?"] or the harrowing dirge *Es ist bestimmt in Gottes Rat* ["It Stands in God's Decrees"], who thinks of the fact that the "foreign" Jew Mendelssohn was the composer? When listening to [Franz] Schubert's *Das Meer erglänzte...* ["The Sea Gleamed..."] or [Robert] Schumann's *Die beiden Grenadiere*

---

15 Translator's note: Iltis misquotes the name of the German town as "Rothenburg *an* der Tauber" (Rothenburg *on* the Tauber, rathern than Rothenburg *above* the Tauber).

["The Two Grenadiers"], who feels the Jewish spirit of the poet Heine? Of course, Heine had to flee from his ungrateful German fatherland to the freer country of France. The German Jews [Giacomo] Meyerbeer [1791–1864] and [Jacques] Offenbach [1819–1880] made their music in France. But Gustav Mahler [1860–1911] wrote his *Lied von der Erde* ["Song of the Earth"] in German Vienna; the Viennese Jew Arnold Schönberg [1874–1951] forged the path of modern music in Germany; and Kurt Weill's [1900–1950] *The Threepenny Opera* [1928] created a new style that began in Germany. The conductor [Hermann] Levi [1839–1900] spread the operas of the anti-Semite Richard Wagner [1813–1883] throughout the world; and the great conductor Bruno Walter [1876–1962] was expelled from present-day Germany but was passionately and enthusiastically celebrated in Vienna and London. The greatest practicing German musicians were Jews: the master pianists Alfred Grünfeld [1852–1924] and Artur Schnabel [1882–1951], and the master violinists Joseph Joachim [1831–1907] and [Arnold Josef] Rosé [1863–1946]. How much poorer would German music be without the Jews! When he was in his 80s, Max Liebermann, the prestigious German painter, had to give up the presidency of the [Prussian] Academy of Arts in Berlin on account of his Jewish descent. Hans von Marées [1837–1887], the great German Impressionist painter, is already dead—otherwise they would have taken away his honor and dignity as well, on account of his Jewish mother. The "half-Jews" or "Jewish bastards" alone—as the new Germany tastefully calls them—have brought such riches to German poetry! Paul Heyse [1830–1914], the great novelist and Nobel Prize laureate, was of Jewish descent. The Egyptologist and epic poet Georg Ebers [1837–1898] had Jewish ancestors. And even Ernst von Wildenbruch [1845–1909], the German nationalist poet from the House of Hohenzollern, had Jewish ancestry. And how much great and genuine art was among the works of Jewish poets that were flung into the pyres by the enraged mobs on May 10, 1933! Jakob Wassermann [1873–1934], the great depicter of people; Georg Kaiser [1878–1945], the pioneer of Expressionism; Lion Feuchtwanger [1884–1958] , the creator of grandiose historical novels; Georg Hermann [1871–1943], the poet of Alt-Berlin; Arthur Schnitzler [1862–1931], the Viennese poet—theirs are among the best German names in the world. And how much greatness and beauty does German theater owe to the Jews! How many great actors, from

[Adolf von] Sonnenthal [1834–1909] to Fritz Kortner [1892–1970] and Elisabeth Bergner [1897–1986], have captivated German audiences on the German stage! How much glory does German theater owe to Otto Brahm [1856–1912] and Max Reinhardt [1873–1943]! All of this, all this impassioned work on the German spirit and for the German spirit is supposed to be nothing—a German Jew is no German at all?

The Jews have made more contributions to the immense achievements of German science in the last 50 years than could possibly be imagined. Let's begin with a representative example, with the loveable science, the "scientia amabilis"—of botany. It is peculiar that the German Jew, the merchant and money-changer, must also be characterized as being the classical German botanist, the bearer of that ideal science. Ferdinand Cohn [1828–1898] in Breslau, Robert Koch's [1843–1910] teacher, was the first to recognize bacteria as pathogens, and thus laid the foundation for modern bacteriology. Julius von Sachs [1832–1897] is the founder of modern plant physiology; Julius Wiesner [1838–1916] of Vienna is the founder of the doctrine of botanical raw materials; [Eduard] Strasburger [1844–1912] is the great researcher of the cell and the cell nucleus; Nathan Pringsheim [1823–1894] recognized the significance of chlorophyll in plants; [Richard] Willstätter [1872–1942], the Nobel Prize laureate, investigated the chemical constitution of chlorophyll; [Paul Friedrich August] Ascherson [1834–1913] knew the flora of the Margraviate of Brandenburg like no other, and his *Synopsis of Central European Flora* [*Synopsis der mitteleuropäischen Flora*] is a classic work; Otto Warburg [1859–1938] did outstanding work in his research of tropical crops, which was a great boon for the German colonies. These are only a few names—if we get rid of the Jews, then German botany must cede first place to other nations!

Just as it did in German botany, Jewish work and the Jewish spirit achieved greatness in German chemistry as well. We'll mention just a few names here: from [Julius Lothar] Mayer [1830–1895], who laid the foundations of modern chemistry with his method of determining molecular weight, through Heinrich Caro [1834–1910], the founder of the amber dye industry, to the Nobel laureate Fritz Haber [1868–1934], who taught us how to transform the nitrogen in the air into fertilizer—quite an illustrious list. Jews and half-Jews [Adolf von] Baeyer

[1835–1917] accounted for most of the founders of the powerful chemical industry conglomerate IG Farben. Similarly, a Jew, Emil Rathenau [1838–1915], founded the powerful electric company AEG [*Allgemeine Elektricitäts-Gesellschaft*]. His son Walther Rathenau [1867–1922], one of the finest and most farsighted Germans, organized Germany's raw material supply during the war, putting himself in service of his homeland in Germany's time of need—and to thank him for this, people with views similar to those of the current masters of Germany killed him ("Shoot down Walter Rathenau, the accursed Jewish swine!"). [Albert] Ballin [1857–1918], the founder of the largest shipping company in the world, the Hamburg America Line—a friend of the German Kaiser and an imperialist!—was a Jew.

German Jews did not merely do business with technology; they also played a massive role in developing the scientific foundations of technology, and in the inventions of the past 50 years. The man who today counts as the most illustrious representative of German science in the entire world, the brilliant mathematician and transformer of the astronomical worldview, Albert Einstein [1879–1955], has been ostracized and exiled from Hitler's Germany, stripped of his honors, and robbed of his possessions. But how pitiful the revenge of the German petit bourgeoisie, who are drunk on power: the universities of all culturally great peoples consider it an honor to receive Albert Einstein as a teacher and researcher. If the pacifist Albert Einstein was expelled from German universities, then Professor James Franck [1882–1964], the Knight of the Iron Cross First Class who was seriously injured in the war, also a Nobel laureate and world-renowned physicist, refused to take up his teaching position in Göttingen under the current government in Germany. "I requested that my supervisory authorities," the brave researcher wrote, "release me from my office. I will try to continue doing scientific work in Germany. We Germans of Jewish descent are being treated as foreigners and enemies of the fatherland. One demands of our children that they grow up with the awareness that they will never be able to call themselves German. Whoever took part in the war is given permission to continue to serve the state. I refuse to avail myself of this privilege…."

The inventions of the German Jew [Emile] Berliner [1851–1929] had a significant impact on the development of the modern telephone; a German

Jew, [Siegfried Samuel] Marcus [1831–1898], built the first automobile before Benz and Daimler; the model of the first steerable airship comes from the Jew David Schwartz [1850–1897], whose patent was taken over by Count [Ferdinand von] Zeppelin [1838–1917]; the blueprints of the first Zeppelin were also designed by a Jewish engineer, [Karl] Arnstein [1887–1974]. Heinrich Hertz [1857–1894], the discover of electrical waves, and thus the actual founder of the modern radio, was also of Jewish origin, as was the famous radio engineer Count [Georg von] Arco [1869–1940]. Robert von Lieben [1878–1913],[16] the Viennese inventor of the amplifying tube and thus of the broadcast receiver, was a German Jew. A full half of the radio has sprouted from the minds of German Jews. To thank them for this, Hitler's hordes use German radio to hurl abuse at German Jews.

The Jew as the doctor of humanity and people! This is a long and powerful history. It begins with Christ and continues through the centuries, yet it also begins with Jewish doctors in Spain and goes on to the great achievements of German-Jewish doctors. If one wanted to be comprehensive here, one would have to fill up volumes with names and deeds. We will focus solely on two small areas: If insulin can be used to cure the awful disease of diabetes today, it is the German Jew [Oskar] Minkowski's [1858–1931] research on the function of the pancreas that has made this possible. And if the dreadful sexually transmitted diseases have today lost a large part of their frightfulness, humanity has German-Jewish doctors to thank for this: [Albert Ludwig] Neisser (1855–1916, Breslau, Prussia) discovered the pathogen of gonorrhea, and [physician] Paul Ehrlich [1854–1915], the great researcher and Nobel laureate, invented Salvarsan, the best remedy for syphilis. With the "Wassermann Test," Professor [August von] Wassermann [1866–1925] devised a method to establish whether a syphilis patient has been fully cured or whether the disease continues to be latent in the blood, and thereby to determine whether a patient can be released from treatment and whether he can marry. Alongside these and other greats, thousands of German-Jewish doctors have given their all to help make and keep the German people healthy—and for this they are now being crippled, chased out of their homeland.

---

16 Translator's note: Iltis gave the wrong abbreviation for his name, "Ä. v. Lieben." There are a few (generally very minor) errors concerning the spellings of various names in this book.

The achievements of the 600,000 German Jews over the past 50 years are so great that they barely seem possible. If these 600,000 people had done in a country of their own what they did for German culture, then the world would have been forced to bow down before such a golden age of the human spirit and creative human activity. Never before in the history of humanity, except perhaps in the advanced civilization of the ancient Greeks, has such a small number of people accomplished so many great deeds for humanity.

If one assumes that the 600,000 Jews, who form 1% of the German population, have contributed to 10% of the overall German artistic, scientific, and economic output of the last one hundred years, then one's estimate would be too low rather than too high. But the Jews have not only given their spirit and their work to Germany, they have also sacrificed their own blood for their homeland. Although a Jew could barely become a reserve officer before the war, and although people endeavored to keep weapons out of Jewish hands, no fewer than 12,000 German Jews died for their ungrateful homeland in the World War. In non-German foreign countries, in Poland, in Hungary, and in the Sudetenland, German Jews often maintained their loyalty to German culture and the German language longer than the non-Jewish Germans did. The cities and country towns of Moravia maintained their German character until very recently thanks solely to the loyalty of Jews. Among the Czechs, a thoroughly liberal nation, anti-Semitic currents have emerged against the Jews primarily as defenders of the German language and culture. Despite economic disadvantages, the Jews remained loyal to Germanness until the period after Hitler's coup. Indeed, even Yiddish, the language of the millions of Jews in Russia and Poland, in London's East End and in New York, is nothing other than the nascent German of the Middle Ages, which the Jews have preserved in the centuries since their departure from their chosen German homeland. Only through the malicious and unjust war of annihilation that the majority of the German people under Hitler have waged against the Jews has the centuries-old and so poorly repaid love that the Jews have for Germany been transformed into hatred.

The German Jews, who have been living and making their homes in Germany for almost a thousand years, have been speaking and thinking German ever since the emancipation. Many of them have better understood and more deeply experienced German culture—the works of the greats poets and thinkers—than large swathes of German workers and peasants have. They went to war for Germany and are bound up with its destiny. They were part of the German people, and disputing their Germanness is an injustice and an act of inhuman cruelty, for they have at least as much right to it as do the descendants of the emigrated French Huguenots, who played and continue to play roles as German nationals. The descendants of the Germans, Czechs, etc. who immigrated to America will be English-speaking Americans by the second generation, or certainly by the third. Why shouldn't the Jews have the right and the possibility to advance in the nation in which they live? The Jews were and still are always grateful to the people that kindly receive them. They felt connected to German culture, as long as it did not persecute them. They have become loyal American citizens, and in the hour of danger they will risk their property and their lives to defend the state. But they also have, through centuries of persecution, a profound sense of the injustices to which they are subjected. Through its brutality, the Third Reich made enemies of the Jews and thus blew up a bridgehead of German culture itself.

People assert that you can always recognize a Jew, and that the Jews must therefore be foreign creatures; and racist authors demonstrate the Jews' "racial-spiritual" foreignness in seemingly profound mystic and mythical treaties, yet provide no facts for their case. But the foreignness of German Jews with respect to other Germans was no greater than the foreignness of the Prussians with respect to the southern Germans or the Austrians! It need only be recalled that before the war "Prussian swine" was just as popular a term in Munich as the term "Jewish swine" was among the anti-Semites! For a racism with an opposing slant, it would be easy to declare the Prussians to be a "foreign-blooded" element in Germany, on the basis of the southern Germans' animosity toward the northern Germans. Every group that is geographically or socially isolated within a people takes on certain characteristics—in terms of their clothing, dialect, lifestyle, etc.—but the individual strains of a people are not declared to be foreign to one another because of this. It can even happen that these differences in language and lifestyle manifest in the facial expressions of the type. In his study *The Franconian Face* [*Das fränkische Gesicht*],

Willy Hellpach [1877–1955] pointed out such relationships and attempted to demonstrate that the Franconian dialect and the Franconian lifestyle lends a peculiar feature to the face of the Franconian and to his nature (similarly to the "Gau type" according to [Egon Freiherr von] Eickstedt [1892–1965]). The Jews too have their own nature, which frequently manifests in their manner of speaking, in their movements, and in their inclinations. For centuries, they were a community of common destiny living in isolation, and their affectations, manner of speaking, etc. were influenced over the centuries by their urban, commercial environment, by the manners and customs of their religion, and so on. It was not to be expected that all of these peculiarities would completely disappear in the three generations that have passed since the emancipation of the Jews and their entry into civil society.

The abnormal occupational stratification of the Jews was caused by their past. For centuries the Jews were denied the right to cultivate the land, just as they were denied membership in the guilds and entry into the civil service career track. The result was that none of the West-European Jews developed any craftsmen communities or farming communities, but rather all of them flowed into the commercial professions, and later, after the emancipation, into the free intellectual professions (doctors, lawyers, writers, etc.). The relatively high percentage of Jews in these professions and their undisputed talent and skill thus incited the envy and hatred of their non-Jewish competitors. This unnatural occupational stratification is one of the main causes of anti-Semitism. But the right consequence would have been to benevolently enable the Jews' return to a normal occupational stratification. The Polish and Russian Jews are showing that the Jews can become craftsmen; the Chalutzim of Palestine are showing that they, like their ancestors, can become farmers. Only through such a policy would a real assimilation of the Jews, and thus a solution to the "Jewish Question", have been possible. This approach is currently being tested in Russia, and despite some difficulties, it seems to being leading to a solution.

The same would have been possible in Germany. Nothing that is being put forward as evidence against this possibility holds any water. The Jews were neither a bad nor a foreign race. The German Jews were also no foreign people, but rather a group of people that had indeed been bound together through religion and shared suffering in the past, but that were ready for and well-suited to assimilation. All the mysterious powers of the Jewish race and people that Nazi mystics write about are unproven and unprovable fantasies—whether one considers these powers to be something positive, as certain Jewish mystics do, or as something negative, as anti-Semites such as Chamberlain and Rosenberg do. If incisive thinking, rapid adaptability, tenacity, and a sense of injustice and unity with oppressed people are more common among the Jews, these are the natural consequences of the hard school of their fate, and not the results of having been mystically chosen by God or the Devil. The Jewish Question should be solved—whether by supporting the Jews in their endeavors to found a homeland and once more become a normal people, or by helping them achieve a normal occupational stratification and assimilate into the people among whom they live. Anti-Semitism provides no solution to the Jewish Question, however, but only serves to aggravate it. And racism, the malicious form of anti-Semitism, is showing the world that the weapon currently turned against the weak group of the Jews can, at any moment, be used to defame other peoples and deprive them of their rights!

Racism is based on the doctrine that different races have different worths. In this evaluation, it is the psychological qualities—the intellectual and moral ones—that naturally play the greatest role. The so-called major races—Europeans, Negroes, Mongols, Pygmies, Australians, etc.—can be easily distinguished from one another based on their physical characteristics. However, there are no even remotely scientifically precise studies on the relationship between physical appearance and certain psychological features. A racially oriented "vocational aptitude test" has not been conducted by science on a larger scale. It has not been determined that certain psychological qualities have a relatively fixed relationship to certain physical qualities of the major races. Neither mathematical talent nor social responsibility, neither poetic fantasy nor the love of truth, is linked to certain races or to certain physical qualities of those races. Black skin does not imply a black soul, and neither frizzy hair nor blue eyes is a sure sign of certain psychological qualities. The Japanese, for example, a Mongolian mixed race, have adopted the entirety of European culture and are now developing just as Europeans do. The modern investigations conducted by [Leo] Frobenius [1873–1938] have shown what a high artistic and material culture pure Negro peoples have developed in the heart of Africa.

German racism, however, does not in any way apply its valuation and classification of races into good, inferior, and bad to the major and easily distinguishable (at least in terms of physical characteristics) racial groups—the European, the Mongolian, the Nigritic, etc.—but rather to the minor and closely related sub-races within the European major strain, to the racial types of the European population. In each European people, the individuals in whom the distinguishing features of different racial types heterogeneously appear are much, much more common than these ideal racial types themselves. Nowhere in the world are the people more strongly mixed than in Europe. The fact that modern culture was created and borne by thoroughly mixed races ought to show those who believe in race that the mixed race is more capable and more valuable than the pure race. But racism completely disregards any contradictions.

The mere physical delimitation of the European races is thus by no means easy—and both crossbreeding and the similarity of racial types with the so-called constitution types blurs the picture even more. Even more difficult is the allocation of certain psychological and intellectual capacities to certain European races.

The fact that certain types repeatedly emerge out of the European racial mixture—for example, the tall Nordic type with its blond hair, light-colored eyes, long face, and long skull, or the stocky Alpine type with its brown skin, brown eyes, round skull, and round face—can be explained by the principles of modern neo-Mendelism: certain distinguishing features, or rather hereditary characteristics, have a tendency toward fixed bonding, toward so-called "coupling." The European races are determined by coupling groups of hereditary characteristics. But the coupling is in no way fixed; it is often broken. The hypothesis of the Nobel laureate [Thomas Hunt] Morgan [1866–1945] explained these frequent broken couplings through peculiar processes in karyokinesis in gametes.

The breaking of couplings thus results, for example, in the fact that the characteristics "blond," "blue-eyed," "dolichocranial," and "tall" are in no way always bound together, but rather combinations such as "blond with dark blue eyes," "blond with a round skull," etc. often arise. On the basis of scientific experience, we can speak much less often of a more-or-less fixed coupling of psychological features to certain physical qualities. It is in no way the case that blond men are better, more capable, or more talented than brunette men. Similarly, dolichocrany does not appear to be in any way linked to special talent or moral superiority. For example, both Australians and Negroes are extremely dolichocranial—two races that, at least according to the racists, certainly cannot be described as being of particularly high quality. On the other hand, the most recent studies by Franz Weidenreich [1873–1948] have proven that the most prominent leaders of the German people—e.g., Goethe, Schiller, Kant, Leibnitz, Luther, and Bismarck, among others—had extremely rounded skulls. From the standpoint of the natural sciences, there is absolutely nothing that indicates that superior psychological features are linked to the physical features of the Nordic race. Nor has it ever been statistically demonstrated that blond people are more intelligent or better than brunette people—or that blond children have better grades in school than brunette children, or that people with narrow faces commit fewer crimes than those with round faces, etc. None of this has been proven—because such differences simply do not exist!

Since neither the natural sciences nor statistics can serve as the basis for the claim that the Nordic race is better than the other European races, one has attempted—ever since Gobineau, Woltmann, and Chamberlain—to bring in evidence through the "cultural-historical" method and to demonstrate that all great cultural achievements should be attributed to the "Aryan," or rather "Nordic," race. It was "determined" that the ancient Greeks and Romans were of Nordic origin. A veritable "hunt for blond hair" of extinct peoples was conducted, with the intention of using tombs and mummies to determine that a "Nordic strain" was the bearer of the great achievements in the ancient Near Eastern cultures, among the Assyrians and Babylonians, but also among the ancient Egyptians. Fritsch, using Egyptian wall paintings, thus attempted to demonstrate that the Libyans (Temenhu) had blond hair. [Julius] Wilser [1888–1949] claimed that he found a blond lock of hair on the skull of the mummy of Ramses. It has also been determined, however, that the Egyptians painted themselves red-brown and their wives yellow on these tomb paintings—one ought to therefore conclude, if these colors are really meant to describe the race, that all male Egyptians were American Indians and that their wives were Chinese (Zollschan)! [Rudolf] Virchow [1821–1902] pointed out that the lock of hair on Ramses's head was very likely once dark, but that it faded over the millennia due to the influence of the external environment. But the racists have never let criticism stand in the way of their fantasies!

The marauding blond Vikings, the magnificent "blond beast" that brought death and destruction to all states and that set up new states—this is the ideal people of the racists. The racists thereby deliberately overlook the fact that the most authentic descendants of these blond barbarians are the present-day Scandinavians, convinced democrats and socialists who reject, and indeed are indignant at, the methods and theories of the Third Reich. The racists also overlook the fact that these most Nordic of people are peaceful and pacifistic. Today's Scandinavians have no tolerance for a modern Viking state. It is also interesting that many of the most prominent Scandinavians—e.g., August Strindberg [1849–1912], Henrik Ibsen [1828–1906], Selma Lagerlöf [1858–1940], Sigrid Undset [1882–1949], and so on—demonstrate a noticeable dark or even Finnish strain.

Racism also attempted to introduce Viking methods into science. Anything that is in any way valuable in the history of humanity is violently claimed as a work of the Nordic race. If one were to read [Hans] Günther's books in France, one would certainly cheerfully receive the discovery announced therein, namely, that all outstanding French generals from the World War actually belong to the Germanic (Nordic) race. In *The Foundations of the 19th Century* [1911], Chamberlain states that even the achievements of the great majority of outstanding Jews are somehow linked to their blond nature. Chamberlain's comical attempt to make a Germanic person out of Christ is well known. The fearless Cardinal [Michael von] Faulhaber's [1869–1952] take on this "experiment" is interesting and relevant; on page 8 of his small book *Judaism, Christianity, and Germany* [*Judentum, Christentum und Germanentum*, 1934] he writes: "Neither does this religious revolution spare the person of Christ. Some wanted to save Christ through a false birth certificate. He was not

131

a Jew at all—he was an Aryan, because Aryans lived in Galilee. But as long as historical sources count more than speculation, the fact cannot be doubted: the first chapter of the first Gospel provides Christ's genealogy with the heading: 'This is the genealogy of Jesus Christ, the son of David, the son of Abraham.' Similarly, the Epistle to the Romans (I.4) states that Christ was a descendant of David. Certainly the Galileans, as a border people, were a mixed people, but Christ was not born in Galilee, he was born in Bethlehem, in the city of David, in the region of the Tribe of Judah, and was officially entered in the civil register as a descendant of David."

Wherever it seems to be absolutely impossible to declare an achievement to be "Nordicly determined," the achievement's value is disputed and disparaged. So it is that we see the persistent racists of the Third Reich fighting against Christianity, whose Jewish origin is indisputable, and rejecting it as un-German and worthless.

Ludwig Woltmann [1871–1907] introduced the method of deducing the Germanic origin of great men—a method that is developed to the point of absurdity in Hans Günther's popular racial picture books. Woltmann tries to explain that the great Italians of the Renaissance, but also the greats among the French, are products of racial mixing with Nordic blood. But as soon as any one of the many cases are examined in a precise and scientific manner, the groundlessness of such claims generally becomes clear.

All of the racists' stories about the Nordic conditionality of the ancient Near Eastern cultures and the cultures of Antiquity are fairy tales.

But even if this claim that a mixing with Nordic blood was the cause of great cultural achievements were true—even then, it would only mean the refutation of a racist dictum. This is because the racists unconditionally demand that the race be kept pure, and they claim that racial mixing, especially the mixing of the Nordic race with others, is a tragedy and a crime. If the great Oriental peoples actually owed their great achievements to an influx of Nordic blood, then we would have proof that precisely the mixture of Nordic blood with Oriental and Near Eastern blood produced valuable results, and therefore that resistance to the "Aryan-Jewish" racial mixture is unjustified! But racism disregards any logical contradictions. It considers science to be a mere political tool; and when it seems expedient, logic is replaced by fairy tales or, in modern terms, by myth. *Mein Kampf* (12th edition, 1932) repeatedly dishes out fairy tales to the reader—not enchanting ones, but rather fairy tales about the terrible effects of miscegenation. "Every animal," we read on page 311/389, "mates only with a representative of the same species. The titmouse seeks the titmouse, the finch the finch,[17] the stork the stork, the field mouse the field mouse, the common mouse the common mouse, the wolf the wolf, etc." The full duplicity and ignorance of racism speaks in these sentences, which speculate on the reader being utterly ignorant. Every thinking person immediately notices that we are here dealing with different species of animals that could never be crossbred, and that when it comes to humans we are dealing with forms within the same type. On page 314/392 of *Mein Kampf*, the consequences of miscegenation, of "blood defilement," are described as follows: "The result of any miscegenation, in brief, is always the following: (a) Lowering of the standard of the higher race, (b) Physical and mental regression, and, with it, the beginning of a slowly but steadily progressive lingering illness. To bring about such a development means nothing less than sinning against the will of the Eternal Creator."

What does science say about the main racist principle that miscegenation is harmful and the cause of the decline of great peoples and cultures?

In his classic work on the Rehoboth Baster people, which was published in 1912, the scholarly protector of German racism, Professor Eugen Fischer, demonstrated that a healthy and capable mixed race can be produced even from the contact of two races as far removed from one another as the South African Hottentots and the Nordic-European Boers. [German Professor Ernest] Rodenwaldt [1878–1965] made similar observations in his study of the so-called *Mestizos from Kisar* [*Die Mestizen auf Kisar*] (1927), who were Dutch-Indian hybrids on the island of Kisar in the Malay Archipelago. The studies by the Americans [Charles] Davenport [1866–1944] and [Morris] Steggerda [1900–1950] on the descendants of the crossing of German farmers and West African Negroes in Jamaica yielded similar results. In all of these cases, there is a great diversity

---

17 Translator's note: Iltis misquoted the original text of *Mein Kampf* here, using the word "Fisch" (fish) instead of "Fink" (finch).

of types, as is to be expected according to the principles of Mendelism, and a diverse mixture of parental traits. As soon as the qualities of the hybrids mutually adapt to one another, new "harmonious" forms emerge—it is likely that many human races arose through such kinds of miscegenation.

One look at the beautiful masculine head of such a Rehoboth Baster from E. Fischer's book (Image 29) and we immediately recognize what kind of evidence the doctrine of the physical inferiority of Basters actually has. In contrast, the physical beauty of racial hybrids is often very conspicuous. It is well known that Count [Richard] Coudenhove-Kalergi [1894–1972], the ideal pioneer of the Paneuropean Movement, came from the marriage of a German[18] aristocrat with a Japanese woman (Image 30). A large number of outstanding men, such as the poet Paul Heyse 1830–1914], the painter Hans von Marées [1837–1887], the chemist [Adolf] von Baeyer [1835–1917], the French poet Anatole France [1844–1924], and finally Charlie Chaplin [1889–1977], come from so-called Jewish-Christian mixed marriages—though it must be noted that such marriages should not be considered miscegenation.

All hypotheses about the physical and psychological inferiority of hybrids fail to withstand scientific scrutiny, and do not hold up to the facts. If mixed-race populations in port cities frequently contain inferior elements, the words of the great German anthropologist Felix von Luschan [1854–1924] explain this phenomenon: "Just like illegitimate children, hybrids are never inferior a priori; they become inferior only if their parents were inferior as individuals." Similarly, the stories about the "psychological conflictedness" and "inner strife" of hybrids should be treated with great caution. If something along those lines really does arise, then the causes for it are not to be sought out in the hybrid, but rather in the puerile racist prejudices of a superstitious environment that rejects anyone who is in the least bit different, and that keeps them at a distance through an "affect of differences" (Freud).

At present, the most powerful states, America, England, France, Germany, etc., are being carried by a racially mixed and crossbred population. All claims by racist historians that would depict the decline of great cultures, peoples, and

---

18 Translator's note: The Count's father was actually Austrian (or Austro-Hungarian).

states as a result of racial mixing, of "racial chaos," are therefore unfounded. The history of the decline of Rome through racial mixing is one of many fairy tales that we come across in the books of the racists. Miscegenation never caused the decline of any race, though it often played a great role in the emergence of new and capable races, and it often, through the felicitous combination of natural abilities, caused the ascendancy of peoples and initiated new cultural epochs. The entire racial legislation of the Third Reich, which aims at "maintaining the purity" of "Aryan" blood and preventing the mixing of Aryans and Jews, contradicts all the findings of science and logic.

Let us summarize. *All attempts at providing a scientific foundation to German racism have failed miserably* (italics added). An Aryan race whose purity is to be maintained and whose ascendancy is to be prepared for does not exist. From the perspective of science, and even from the perspective of racist science, an Aryan legislation is therefore nonsense. The German people consist of a mixture of different racial types. Indeed, the achievements of the German people may be attributable precisely to their racial "diversity." *The different races within a body of people can be compared to the voices in an orchestra—the richer the mixture, or the more polyphonic the melody, the richer the culture will be* (italics added).

In his *Race Theory of the German People*, the founder of German racism, Hans Günther, lists seven major races and seven minor races out of which the population of Germany is composed. If one asserts that only the Nordic racial component of the German people is valuable, then that would mean that at least three quarters of all Germans are racially inferior. If one asserts that all the German people are "Aryan" and confers a specific value to each of their racial components, then one cannot consider the Jewish population, which is composed of closely related racial elements, to be racially inferior. The Jews constitute a mixed race that is composed of almost the same racial elements that play the primary role in the population of southern and southeastern Europe. If there is a special Jewial type that is particularly conspicuous in places where large numbers of Jews have lived together in cramped spaces for a long time, then that type is determined not by race, but by the centuries-old urban environment, the ghetto. It is a supreme injustice when today's anti-Semites reproach the Jews for the qualities that created the ghetto, into which the anti-Semites forced the Jews from the very beginning. From the perspective of science, in any case, it is entirely unfounded to characterize the Jews as a foreign element within the European population.

No clear link can be established between special psychological values and certain physical racial qualities. Neither blondness nor dolichocrany is necessarily linked to superior moral or intellectual qualities. People from the Nordic racial type have certainly achieved great things—but so too have people from the other racial types of the German people, and also people from the Mediterranean-Oriental and Dinaric-Near Eastern type, which is characteristic for the southern European people group as well as the Jewish people group. From the perspective of science, legal bias toward the Nordic race is just as unjustified as legal discrimination against the Jewish race. The legislation pertaining to Jews in Hitler's Germany is nothing more than an act of political despotism.

It cannot be scientifically proven that the mixing of different European racial types with one another and with the related racial types of the Jewish population group produces physically or psychologically negative results. On the contrary, the results of objective research, especially Eugen Fischer's studies of the Rehoboth Basters, indicate that when merely the parents themselves, as individuals, have good physical and psychological qualities, then the descendants from the miscegenation also become capable, full-fledged people. German legislation forbids unions between German Jews and other Germans, and deprives the children of such unions of their rights. This anti-Semitic legislation cannot in any way be based on science.

But in the Third Reich, the scientific basis, which was still the norm during the struggle against the Republic, has already been abandoned. While Günther still sought to provide scientific justification for the superiority of the Nordic race and the inferiority of the Alpine and Jewish race, Alfred Rosenberg, the prophet of the Third Reich, took refuge behind myth. The "myth of blood" was announced. In its name, Rosenberg's own race was elevated to heaven, while the other race was turned into an object of scorn.

The findings of modern science indicate that blood does not divide the human races, but rather unifies them. It has been known for quite some time that in blood transfusions, i.e., the transfer of foreign human blood after the loss of blood, not just any blood can be used, since in many cases clotting can result, and with it serious health problems. The research of R. Kraus, Landsteiner, Shattock, and others have shed light on this phenomenon. Blood serum contains compounds that, in foreign blood, cause blood corpuscles to stick together and "clump," so-called "agglutination." It was further determined that we can divide people into four blood groups according to their blood, or rather according to the behavior of their blood serum, and indeed, according to the studies of recent years, into a much larger number of such blood groups. Every person can be classified under one of these blood groups, which have been designated as group O, group A, group B, and group AB. For a blood transfusion, we can generally only use blood from people who are in the same blood group as the patient without causing harm.

Of course, the attempt was immediately made to exploit the science of blood groups in order to distinguish human races. It would naturally be ideal for the racists if one could immediately distinguish the Nordic race from the inferior Jewish or Alpine race through the former's noble blood. Unfortunately, science has demonstrated the opposite! Blood group research has shown that people with the same blood behavior, e.g. those who belong to blood group A, can be found in the Mongolian race as in the Negrid and the Nordic. If blood behavior were decisive, then these people from very different races would have to be closer to one another than to people of their own race who belong to other blood groups. Only the percentage in which the individual blood groups occur is different among different races and nations. Thus, blood group A is more common in Western Europe, blood group B in East Asia, blood group O in America. It seems here that geographic circumstances play a greater role than race relations.

In the overall population of Germany, the following division of the four blood groups was determined though large-scale statistics:

O	A	B	AB
39.0%	43.2%	12.5%	5.3%

Among Jews from Berlin, the corresponding figures are:

42.1%	41.1%	11.9%	4.9%

In contrast, among the Mongolian inhabitants of China the blood groups are divided as follows:

26.7%	26.6%	38.2%	8.5%

It is thus clear that the percentage ratio of the blood groups of Jews from Berlin is only very slightly different from that of the overall population of Germany. In contrast, the Chinese demonstrate a much greater occurrence of blood group B. But even in this very different major race, we have the same four blood groups that are present among Europeans.

The Czech anthropologist [Vojtěch] Suk [1879–1967] conducted extensive studies on the behavior of different human races in relation to their blood groups. Among other things, he examined more than 3000 people of different European racial types in Brno, in Moravia, in relation to their blood behavior, and determined that in this large sample 28.8% belonged to blood group O, 44% to blood group A, 18.2% to blood group B, and 9% to blood group AB. Neither Suk nor any other author was able to determine a clear and plain distinction with regard to blood groups between the so-called European races and the Jewish people group. Blood unites—blood does not separate the human races! The expression "blood ties," which are supposed to unite people of the same race, is an empty phrase. There is no German blood, there is no Jewish blood. Science says this—whereas racism insists on its "blood myth."

We are not against myths and fairy tales—it would impoverish humanity if these flowers were to spoil under the icy breath of reason. But making myths and fairy tales the foundation of political action is as dangerous as it is reprehensible. All human justice, all mutual understanding and respect, and even the existence of the complicated social organism of modern states, are based on the recognition of objective experience that is valid for all people, and on science and respect for science. Arbitrary myth can at best serve as the foundation of violence. But: "All who draw the sword will die by the sword."[19]

---

19   Translator's note: *Matthew* 26:52 (cited from the New International Version of the Bible).

RACISM IN POLITICS

The science of human races, which aims to know the facts and explore the truth, lays no foundations whatsoever for the claims that we owe the origin of human culture only to certain individual races, that, in addition to the valuable human races, worthless human races also exist, and that only the valuable races have the right to rule. The racism that makes these claims is not a science but rather a dangerous and malicious weapon intended to procure advantages for one's own race, one's own people, and to denigrate other races and deprive them of rights. This is openly acknowledged in present-day Germany. There, it has been officially proclaimed that science only has significance if and when it serves the nation. It is not supposed to be objective, but consciously subjective and nationalist. "Instinctive" myth has taken the place of objective science.

Just how the racist politicians advance with this insidious and extremely dangerous weapon, with this "intellectual poison gas," against all peoples and people groups that they hope to murder either economically or politically will be elaborated with the use of quotations from both of the major works of German political racism.

Racism is the foundation of Hitler's *Mein Kampf* (we are quoting from the 12th edition, Munich 1932, which was published before Hitler's coup). "The question of race," we read on page 371/470, "not only furnishes the key to world history, but also to human culture as a whole." "In this world," we read on page 428/582, "human culture and civilization are inseparably bound up with the existence of the Aryan. His dying-off or his decline would again lower upon this earth the dark veils of a time without culture." The author of *Mein Kampf* does not seem to have read the theorists of his own party. If he had read them, he would not only know that science unconditionally refuses to use the term "Aryan" in relation to race, but also that even the racist pseudoscientists, such as the court racist [Hans] Günther, admit and even stress that while Aryan languages may exist, there are no Aryan races, nor have there ever been any. A purely Aryan language is, for example, spoken by the Armenians today—in racial terms, they are the people most closely related to the Jews. In contrast, the "awakening" Hungarians cannot in any way be characterized as Aryans, since they speak a non-Aryan Ugric-Tatar language.

In the linguistic usage of National Socialist politics, the word "Aryan" has been given the meaning of "non-Jew"—everything that is not Jewish is Aryan. A German racist will become embarrassed if he is asked about the race of the American Indians. He will likely explain that the American Indians must be Aryans, since they're not Jews! Such logical sleights of hand have already been used in official circles. After Hitler's coup, when "public rage" at "racial defilement" began to also turn against the Japanese living in Berlin, the good race of the Japanese was officially confirmed—they were named Aryans free of charge, as it were.

We have established that science, even German national science, denies the existence of an "Aryan race." It must be emphatically stressed that terms such as "Aryan paragraph," "Aryan descent," etc. are utterly meaningless.[20]

"The foreign policy of a national state," we read in *Mein Kampf* (p. 728/935), "is charged with guaranteeing the existence on this planet of the race embraced by the state."

But Professor Günther, the racist expert of the National Socialists, expressly establishes that the German people, i.e., the substratum of the German national state, are composed of seven major races and five minor races,[21] of which some are glorified while others are belittled. And in *Mein Kampf* itself,

---

20 Translator's note: The term "Aryan paragraph" refers to any legislation, real estate deeds, or statutes of organizations or corporations that reserve certain key rights (such as membership, employement, or residence) to people of Aryan descent, thereby excluding Jews and people of Jewish descent from such rights. Germany's "Law for the Restoration of the Civil Service" from April 1933, which allowed for any civil servants (including tenured ones) who were not of Aryan descent to be dismissed from their posts, is perhaps the most infamous example of an Aryan paragraph.

21 Translator's note: On page 67 of this text, Iltis states that Günther lists seven major and seven (not five) minor races.

we read the following six pages later (p. 734/942): "... the German people, super-individualistically disintegrated by its jumbled blood." Where, then, can we find "the race united by the state?" It must be the case that the future program of the "Nordification [*Vernordung*] of the German people" is already being anticipated—which would of course require that the inferior southern Germans be exterminated, and that all of Germany be reserved solely for the Prussian-Nordic master race.

Therefore: There is no Aryan race, nor has there ever been one—the German people are a thoroughly hybrid racial mix—and yet the author of *Mein Kampf* along with all the present-day lords of Germany are constructing their famous race laws, indeed their entire worldview, on the foundation of the superiority of this non-existent Aryan race and on the unity of a non-existent German race.

We repeatedly come across this contradiction in *Mein Kampf*. The German people, whose great deeds of humanity are praised in the most glowing terms, are composed of a mixture of very different races. This is explicitly acknowledged in *Mein Kampf*. "Unfortunately, our German people are no longer based on a uniform nucleus. [...] On the contrary, the blood-poisoning that affected our national body, especially since the Thirty Years' War, led not only to a decomposition of our blood but also of our soul. [...] The racial elements are situated differently, not only territorially but also within the same territory. Ostic people stand at the side of Nordic people, Dinaric people at the side of Ostics, Westerners at the side of both, and in between there are hybrids" (p. 436/597–598). Within this racial mixture, the Nordic-Prussian racial type is praised as being particularly valuable. "This is the blessing of the failure of complete mixture: that even today we still have in our German national body great stocks of Nordic-Germanic people who remain unblended, in whom we may see the most valuable treasure for our future" (p.438/600). And farther on, we read: "The German Reich, as a state, should include all Germans, not only with the task of collecting from the people the most valuable stocks of racially primal elements and preserving them, but also to lead them, gradually and safely, to a dominating position" (p. 439/601). We can see which elements are to rule over the inferior southern and central German races from the explanations of Alfred Rosenberg, the party's theorist: "Beyond this purely anti-Semitic practical application, racial hygiene must be maintained, as well as the great goal—the greatest goal—of the northering of our people in the sense of Nordic thought" (Alfred Rosenberg [1893–1946], "The Program of the NSDAP [National Socialist German Workers' Party]," p. 44). The German people are thus supposed to become Nordic—similarly to how the various Ferdinands [Catholic monarchs] wanted to make them Catholic 300 years ago! Only those who are blond, blue-eyed, slender, and narrow-skulled have the right to rule in Germany. But what is to become of today's leaders, propaganda chiefs, etc., who are neither blond nor blue-eyed nor tall, and who in no way correspond to the ideal image of the Nordic race? And finally: Will the "racially inferior" Austrian and Bavarian peasants, as well as the "bastardized" Viennese workers, always agree to such a role and to restrictions on the number of their descendants in favor of a Prussian-Nordic master people? The world does not agree with racism in its evaluation of the Prussian-Nordic people and the southern-German-Alpine people. Austrians, Swabians, Franconians, Rhinelanders, i.e., the least Nordic strains, are more popular in the world than the ubiquitously hated Prussians, even with the latter's celebrated efficiency.

The fact that the German people, despite its mixed race and hybridization, exhibits the greatest achievements in all domains somehow provides absolutely no reason for racism to approve of racial mixing and hybridization—for logic is of no consequence to racism. Instead, racial mixing is declared a crime, is declared "blood defilement." "Peoples that bastardize themselves, or permit themselves to be bastardized, sin against the will of eternal providence" (*Mein Kampf*, p. 359/452). "The loss of the purity of blood alone destroys inner happiness forever; it eternally lowers man, and never again can its consequences be removed from body and mind" (p. 359/452).

These grand dogmas put forth with such certainty about the consequences of miscegenation, "defilement of blood," or "racial defilement," as they are tastefully named in the Third Reich, make only one mistake: they contradict the facts established by science. Eugen Fischer, the director of the Kaiser Wilhelm Institute in Berlin and the first rector of the University of Berlin under the National Socialist regime—therefore certainly an unsuspicious witness!—not only determined in his famous studies on the Rehoboth Basters that a physically and mentally capable hybrid people emerged even from the crossbreeding of Dutch people and Hottentots—two certainly very different races—he also, shortly before Hitler's rise to power (spring 1933), summarized our general knowledge of miscegenation in a presentation at the Kaiser Wilhelm Society and determined that, at least as far as Germany is concerned, the highest artistic and scientific achievements were and still are by racially mixed people. We need only look at the pictures of Goethe, Luther, and Beethoven (Images 17, 18, 19) to recognize that these greatest of Germans were hybrids. And the famous American plant breeder and biologist Luther Burbank [1849–1926]—to cite another prominent name—writes: "Experience has shown that the best and most competent type of person is the hybrid. This is true in relation to almost all the great people of history, just as it is true in relation to the races themselves." According to science, miscegenation is thus in no way dangerous. On the contrary: The greatest geniuses and the most capable peoples sprouted from miscegenation!

Despite this scientifically established state of affairs, we read the following in *Mein Kampf* (p. 434/604): "Every race-crossing leads necessarily sooner or later to the decline of the mixed product." The entire political argumentation of racism is built on such incorrect claims about the dreadful effect of miscegenation. This is how Hitler, with his antipathy to racial mixing, justifies his raging hatred for Vienna, for the city that resisted him in the murky beginnings of his career. "I detested the conglomerate of races," we read in *Mein Kampf* (p. 135/160), "that the realm's capital manifested. [...] To me the big city appeared as the personification of racial defilement...." In contrast, Munich appeals to him, although every race researcher would tell him that the people of Munich are neither more Nordic nor of purer race that the people of Vienna. But we still read the following in *Mein Kampf* (p. 138/163): "A German city! What a difference as compared with Vienna! It made me sick only to think back to that racial Babylon...."

This is how Hitler passes judgment on Vienna, on the home of Beethoven and Schubert, on the city that has certainly made more—and more noble—contributions to German culture than any other!

But the Viennese are not the only ones who appear as inferior hybrids according to the racial doctrine of the Nazis.

The doctrine of "racial defilement" was primarily used to underpin the smear campaign against France. The French are a "Jewish-Negro" hybrid people and are therefore inferior and degenerate. Nazi logic disregards the small and inconsequential fact that this "degenerate" people won the Battle of the Marne. *Mein Kampf* has no end of words for the "bastardization and negroization" with which France is threatening all of Europe. "What France, spurred by its own vengefulness, methodically led by the Jew, is doing in Europe today, is a sin against the existence of white humanity, and someday will inspire against that nation all the avenging spirits of a knowledge that will have recognized race pollution as the original sin against mankind" (*Mein Kampf*, p. 705/908). "Exactly for this reason France is, and remains by far, the most terrible enemy. This people, which is constantly becoming more negrofied, constitutes, by its tie with the aims of Jewish world domination, a grim danger for the existence of the European white race. For infection in the heart of Europe through Negro blood on the Rhine corresponds equally to the sadistic perverse vengefulness of this chauvinistic hereditary enemy of our people, and to the ice-cold plan of the Jews to begin bastardizing the European continent at its core...." (*Mein Kampf*, p. 704/907–908). Such brutally mendacious quotations, whose number could be multiplied at will, are characteristic of Nazi mentality. The claim that the French are polluting the Rhine through Negro blood out of vengefulness is a lie; the claim that the Jews want to bastardize the European continent is also a lie; and the claim that a race degenerates through crossbreeding is a lie as well. *Mein Kampf* declares the French race to be polluted—but the majority of all people see the true danger of pollution in the spread of the brutal Prussian spirit.

If we encounter unadorned brutality in *Mein Kampf*—it would be a worthwhile task, for example, to determine the number of swear words in it—then Alfred Rosenberg [1843–1946], the theorist and foreign policy head of the Hitler movement, endeavors to represent the finer literary-philosophical note in his large work *The Myth of the Twentieth Century* [1930].[22] But the same spirit

---

22 Iltis's note: Alfred Rosenberg, *Der Mythus des 20. Jahrhunderts*, 3rd edition, Munich: Hohe-neichenverlag, 1932 [1930].

of violent mendacity shines through the whitewash of mystical-metaphysical fantasies, through the mess of hollow phrases. Facts are no obstacles to Alfred Rosenberg's philosophy of history. According to Rosenberg, the God of the Nordic Greeks is Apollo, and the God of the Nordic Germanic people is "Christ, the hero with the spear." The Germanic man is "Luciferian," the Jew "Satanic"—and more such nonsense. The "racial-psychological" worldview, the old racism, shines forth through such hollow phrases, which are delivered with great emotion. "Science too is a consequence of blood. Everything that we today call abstract science is a result of Germanic creative powers" (*Myth*, p. 135). Rosenberg's historiography demonstrates what this Germanic science looks like. The greatest people of world history are the marauding Vikings: "The Viking emerges in history with an astounding high-handedness" (*Myth*, p. 145). After an analysis of the Viking's achievements, Herr Rosenberg comes to the comically grotesque conclusion that, "when seen from this perspective, the Viking is actually the civilized man, whereas the aesthetically perfected Greek man of late Antiquity is the backward, un-centered barbarian" (*Myth*, p. 167). The Germanic knight and the Prussian officer are in alignment with the Nordic Viking. However, it is Friedrich II of Prussia, whose reign witnessed ceaseless war in Germany, who represents the highest ideal for the Nazis. "The spirit of Friedrich the Great today appears as an untamable force of nature among the German people" (*Myth*, p. 214). "His life is the greatest, most authentic German history, and anyone who tries to distort the figure of the Fridericus [Frederic the Great] with spiteful comments appears to us today as a miserable rogue" (*Myth*, p. 209). In his calmly investigative book, Werner Hegemann [1891–1936] has shown us the *Fridericus*, whose inner Prussian brutality repeatedly breaks through the thin varnish of culture and literature, and for whom the following phrase, which he shouted at his flinching soldiers, is characteristic: "Dogs, do you want to live forever?"

For Herr Rosenberg, anyone who dares to criticize the figure of the Fridericus is a rogue. To most Europeans, however, the real rogue would be one who insults the French Revolution, that great heroic struggle of oppressed humanity, and who denigrates the French people—as Herr Rosenberg does. "The French Revolution of 1789 was only a single large collapse without creative ideas, and today we are experiencing its decay" (*Myth*, p. 553). Only demented petit-bourgeois were enthusiastic about the French Revolution (*Myth*, p. 117). According to Rosenberg, the best remnants of the noble Germanic master race of France were eradicated by the French Revolution: "... the Jacobinic mob dragged anyone who was slender and blond to the scaffold" (*Myth*, p. 118). In the words of Rosenberg, it is inferiority that reigns in present-day France. In terms of racial politics, it is here extremely important to stress that the racial type that today determines French life (Doumergue, Herriot, Briand, etc.) has nothing to do with the image of ancient France, but rather should be classified as the descendants of a different racial stratum (the Ostic-brachycephalic) than the earlier Nordic-Westic-dolichocranial. For Herr Rosenberg, Herriot's figure in particular seemed to be the embodiment of incompetence. "An archetype of a hero as a stocky, broad-shouldered, bow-legged, thick-necked, and flat-browed person itself belongs in the realm of impossibility, where types such as Herriot will wash up to the surface" (*Myth*, p. 296).

[For Rosenberg] France was once blond and German, today it is degenerate. But a few blond Frenchmen must still be around, otherwise they would not have been able to win the World War. "In 1914, Germany faced this power of northern France, which was still strong (Normandy was always considered a 'small Germany' in the Middle Ages and beyond[23]). However, it was not prominent personalities with blood ties to the Germans who now had control over this power, but rather Rothschild bankers and other financial powers who were racially related to them. And with them people like Fallières, Millerand, or the Alpine impotence of Herriot and company. Thus it is only today that the last valuable blood is seeping away. Entire regions in the south have died out and are now drawing in the people of Africa, as Rome once did. An increasingly decaying population is flooding into Paris, around the Notre Dame. Negroes

---

23 Translator's note: The German text simply reads "in der Ketzerzeit" here, which literally means "in the age of heretics." It is not an expression that I have ever heard of, but I believe it refers to the Reformation movement within the Catholic Church (during the Renaissance), and possibly to the period prior to that (i.e., the Late Middle Ages), when no small number of heretics were being put to death.

and mulattoes are linking arms with white women, a purely Jewish quarter is emerging with new synagogues. South American, mestizo-like posers are polluting the race of the still-beautiful women who are attracted to Paris from all over France. We are thus currently experiencing something that has already unfolded in Athens, Rome, and Persepolis. Therefore a close relationship with France, to say nothing of the political-military aspect, is equivalent to a marriage with someone afflicted with the plague. The call here is rather for the following: isolation of the European West; border closures on account of anthropological features; a Nordic-European coalition; cleansing the European motherland of the germs of Africa and Syria that are spreading out from central France" (*Myth*, p. 119).

The man who is attacking France's honor in this way is no ordinary soldier of the Nazi army—he [Alfred Rosenberg] is the Third Reich's head of foreign policy! And the passage quoted above is not the only one in which Rosenberg heaps scorn on the France of the great revolution, the France of Napoleon, the France of the Battle of the Marne, as an inferior, degenerate pariah state. "France today is at the forefront of the mongrelization of Europe" (*Myth*, p. 633). "Thanks solely to the policies of Rothschild's Republic, which is racially polluting the West with the help of all of Africa, that Republic is emerging as a first-class danger for all of Europe" (*Myth*, p. 626). "France will thus be sustained by an instinctive racial fear—a result of racial defilement—that will always be part of any at best externally victorious bastard. Thus the still-prevalent, trembling fear of Germany, which was overcome with the help of the entire planet" (*Myth*, p. 119).

These quotations all clearly demonstrate the meaning of racist ideology. That ideology is a dangerous and malicious tool for denigrating and "dealing with" one's political and economic opponents. Like France itself, France's allies are denied racial honor. If France is "degenerate and mongrelized," then the Czechs and Poles are uncultured and worthless half-savage peoples who have no right to European soil. Along these lines, Alfred Rosenberg's portrayal of Hussitism is typical. After Rosenberg openly praises the Huguenot movement as the struggle of the Nordic man against Roman Unitarianism, he continues with typical Nazi logic: "The preceding requires a counterpart, however, so as to not allow any superficial assessment. [...] For example, the history of the Hussites. [...] The racially foreign Alpine-Dinaric nature appeared here, which manifested in uncultured savageness combined with awful superstition" (*Myth*, p. 123). "The one-eyed Zizka of Trocnov (whose head in the Prague National Museum identifies him as Ostic-Near-Eastern) was the first expression of this all-destructive Taborite movement, to which the Czechs owe both the eradication of the Germanic powers that were still present in them and the repelling of their truly Slavic powers...." "As if driven by a Near-Eastern madness, Taborite zealots are rising up...." (*Myth*, p. 124). "... Taboritism cost the Czech nature virtually all the unique civilized powers it possessed. Since then, this people has been uncreative and owes its later cultural recovery to the recently inrushing German formal powers. To this day, savageness combined with cowardice remains a characteristic of the Czech nature (Hasek's 'Svejk' is the authentic national hero of this incompetent nation)" (*Myth*, p. 125–126). "This view of Czech history is extremely instructive for all subsequent racist historical research and teaches the sharp distinction between freedom and 'freedom.' [...] Attributing an external 'freedom' to Czechs, Poles, and Levantines today means surrendering oneself to racial chaos" (*Myth*, p. 126).

In these quotations by Rosenberg we can recognize the "absolute, impudent, and unilateral stubbornness" that is recommended in *Mein Kampf*[24] as an effective means of agitation. The Czechs are the nation of [Jan Amos] Komensky [John Amos Comenius, 1592–1670], the first good European and the great educator; they are the nation of [Tomáš] Masaryk [1850–1937], the powerful revolutionary, the "philosopher on the throne"; they are the nation of [Bedřich] Smetana [1824–1884] and [Antonin] Dvorak [1841–1904], whose music is considered among the most noble of humanity's achievements. But according to Rosenberg, "savageness combined with cowardice" is "a characteristic of the Czech nature"—therefore it is madness to grant them freedom and their own land, all the more so when the Third Reich lays claim to that land.

---

24 Translator's note: Iltis does not provide a page number here, but this citation is from page 201 of the German edition that he has been citing, and from page 238 of the English that I have been using (I have modified the English translation).

The quotations from *Mein Kampf* and from *Myth* have shown us what racism means. Racism is intellectual poison—through poisonous lies, it clouds peoples' minds and whips them into a frenzy of theft and murder. But we have not only read this in quotations, we have experienced the bloody reality of the ends to which German National Socialism makes use of racism. The fate of the German Jews demonstrates to what ends racism is used.

The Jews are a mixed race like the Germans: their three most important racial elements—the Near-Eastern-Dinaric, the Oriental-Mediterranean, and the Nordic—are virtually the same ones that play the major role in both the European and the German racial mixture. And yet a hysterical hatred for the Jews, a brutal anti-Semitism, is being built on an alleged racial contrast between Jews and Germans. There are many Jews who are, in racial terms, overwhelmingly Nordic (Images 20 and 26), and there are others in whom the Nordic element appears bound up with the Mediterranean element—there are many Germans who are racially Alpine or Ostic, and therefore much farther removed from the ideal of the Nordic race than the aforementioned Jews. But the fact that the Jewish mixed race differs only slightly from the European mixed races does not prevent the racists from declaring that the Jewish racial mixture is particularly bad, and that the psychological qualities of the Jews are particularly dangerous. Psychological qualities cannot be measured like physical ones, which leaves a lot of room for hypotheses and suspicions. The Jews demonstrate the same racial mixture as large parts of the population of southern and central Europe. But if a racial contrast does not exist, then one must be constructed. For such a contrast is needed in order to be able to wage an economic and political struggle against the Jews.

The Jews [they argue] have poisoned the world—they are the originators of both Christianity and Freemasonry, of both capitalism and Marxism—the Jews must be annihilated!

"Anti-Semitism is, to a certain extent, the emotional substructure of our movement. Every National Socialist is an anti-Semite," we read in the paper, "The Program of the NSDAP [National Socialist German Workers Party] and the Worldviews it is Based On" [*Das Programm der NSDAP und seine weltanschaulichen Grundgedanken*] by Dr. Gottfried Feder [1883–1941] (p. 30). "From this substructure there emerges," Feder writes in the same paper, "the fundamental third thesis of the National Socialist program—'The elimination of the Jews and all non-Germans from all positions of authority in public life.' This demand is so self-evident for us National Socialists that it requires no further elucidation. For those who have not grasped at least the foundations of race theory, however, it is impossible to give a concise and convincing explanatory statement. Anyone who sees in the Jew merely a German citizen with Jewish beliefs rather than a foreign and strictly self-contained people with parasitic qualities, cannot understand the imperative nature of this demand. Anyone who claims that a kohlrabi plant that happened to grow in a strawberry patch is in fact a strawberry bush, or who believes that strawberries can be harvested from it through gentle coaxing, is mistaken...." (Dr. [Gottfried] Feder, ibid., p. 43).

Such are the foundations of National Socialist race theory: The Jew is a kohlrabi, the German a strawberry. If science cannot establish a significant racial difference between the German Jews and the other Germans, then such a comparison must convince every logical thinking person that all Jewish civil servants, all Jewish doctors, lawyers, artists, journalists, etc. must be chased out of their jobs, that all Jewish businesses must be boycotted, and that all Jewish citizens—of whom no less than 12,000 gave their lives for Germany in the World War—must be insulted and abused, robbed and deported!

The race of the Jews is neither foreign nor bad. The Jews have their traits, their good and bad qualities, like every other people group. But these traits have much less to do with race than with the ghetto and the centuries-long environment of oppression. Despite their hard, tragic fate, the capacity of this ancient people has not been broken, but rather been increased. Through their "Holy Books," the Jews of ancient Palestine provided the foundation for Christian civilization. The cultural achievement that was present in the overcoming of polytheism and the magical worldview, as well as in the introduction of social legislation (the weekly day of rest, etc.), is significant not only for religious Christians, however. "Whoever does not believe in divine inspiration," Cardinal [Michael von] Faulhaber writes on page 76 of his courageous book *Judaism, Christianity, and Germany*, "and does not accept these books as God's word and God's revelation must consider the people of Israel as the greatest people in world history." And just as the ancient Jews, through Moses and Christ, laid the intellectual foundations for the Christian world, so have the modern Jews, through Marx and Lassalle, laid the intellectual foundations for the socialist world. But to the racists, the Jews are an inferior race. The fact that 14 of the 140 Nobel Prize laureates—or 10%— from all peoples and races are of Jewish descent while Jews comprise barely 1% of humanity poses no difficulty to racist logic and no obstacle to racist brutality. It is of no help that the small number of German Jews—1% of Germany's population—have, through unique intellectual and artistic achievements, made significant contributions to overall German culture. None of this bothers the racists—the Jew is banished!

In the legislation pertaining to the Jews from the years 1933 to 1935, the Nazis' unrestrained hatred for the Jews has been raging.

We know that the German people represent a thoroughly hybrid racial mixture; we know that much greater racial differences can arise among non-Jewish Germans than between Germans and Jews; and we know that the concept "German blood" is a fantastical entity that does not correspond to anything in reality. And yet the first part of §2 of the "Law on Nationality and Reich Citizenship" [*Gesetzes über Staatsangehörigkeit und Reichsbürgerschaft*] states: §2, Part 1, "Only the national subject of German or related blood is a citizen of the Reich…" In the "Special Provisions for Jews" that belong to this law, the following is declared: §1, Part 1, "Marriages between Jews and citizens of German or related blood are forbidden. Marriages performed in spite of this are null and void. […] §2, Extramarital relations between Jews and citizens of German or related blood are forbidden. […] §5, Part 1, Whoever violates the ban of §1 will be given a prison sentence. […] Part 2, Any man who violates §2 will be given a prison sentence."

There is no Aryan race, there is no "German or related blood"—and yet all German race legislation is based on these mendacious concepts. The Jews make up 1% of the population in Germany—they are a defenseless minority at the mercy of the violent acts and insults of the rulers. The German race laws through which the Jews are abused are built on lies. And racism, the worldview of the Nazis, is also built on lies. A system can indeed be erected through lies— but it cannot be maintained through lies; sooner or later it must shamefully collapse. Then its representatives will be exposed to the world as bloodstained, violent liars.

The German persecution of the Jews from March to April 1933, the brutal crackdown against the defenseless Jewish minority, the disgraceful legislation pertaining to the Jews—these are showing the world what lies in store for whomever is put into the hands of today's rulers. They are a warning to Germany's neighboring states and peoples: When the time comes, your racial inferiority will be proven by German professors, will be felt out by the ones who proclaimed the "myth of blood!"

Their race must be inferior, since one needs their land, their soil and territory. Alfred Rosenberg, the Third Reich's head of foreign policy, explains the third demand of the National Socialist Program ("We demand land and territory (colonies) to feed our people and for our population surplus to settle in") with the following sentence: "It goes against all natural order that 36 million French people have more land at their disposal than 63 million Germans, that a Russian has 20 times more land than a German. This unnatural ratio will come to an end in a way that has always befallen all things in history: through the national struggle for power. Here too, it is a matter of achieving our life necessities or sinking" (Alfred Rosenberg, "Nature, Principles, and Goals of the NSDAP" [*Wesen, Grundsätze und Ziele der NSDAP*], Munich 1930, p. 16).

In *Mein Kampf*, clear consequences are derived from these principles: "Because we must at last become entirely clear about this: the German people's irreconcilable mortal enemy is and remains France." That's what we read on page 699/902 of *Mein Kampf*. France is the main obstacle to Germany's "eastern policy," through which Germany seeks to gain more land "in the east." "But if we talk about new soil and territory in Europe today, we can think primarily only of Russia and its vassal border states. Fate itself seems to give us a tip at this point. [...] The giant realm in the east is ripe for collapse" (*Mein Kampf*, p. 743/950–2).

But if Russia too is only a cadaver from which pieces can be broken off at will, France must first be dealt with. That alone will pave the way for greater Germany, of which Hitler paints a grandiose portrait for us: "Only when this is fully understood in Germany so that the German nation's will to live is no longer allowed to waste itself in purely passive defensiveness, but is drawn together for a decisive, active settlement with France, and is thrown into a final, decisive battle for the vastest German final goals: only then will it be possible to bring to a conclusion our eternal struggle with France, in itself so fruitless; on condition, of course, that Germany really sees in France's annihilation merely a means of subsequently and finally giving our nation a chance to expand elsewhere. Today we are eighty million Germans in Europe! That foreign policy will be acknowledged as correct only if, a bare century from now, two hundred and fifty million Germans are living on this continent, and then not squeezed together as factory coolies for the rest of the world, but as peasants and workers mutually guaranteeing each other's life by their productivity" (*Mein Kampf*, p. 766/978–979).

Herr Alfred Rosenberg declares himself ready, however, to most mercifully allow a subjugated France to live, under certain conditions. "Incidentally, an intelligent French nature would have been able," he writes in *Myth*, p. 627, "to bring about a recovery of its country. Of course, no longer on the basis of its former Nordic heritage, but rather according to its Alpine-Westic racial character: if it, in recognition of natural biological necessity, renounced dominance in Europe, allowed Poland, Czechoslovakia, and the others from the so-called Little Entente to fall, purposefully took on the elimination of Jews and Negroes, and contented itself with the borders determined by its population. This France could dedicate itself to its culture without any obstacles from Germany."

Germany would potentially allow such a small French state to live—but in no way would it do the same with the "Czechs, Poles, and the others from the so-called Little Entente."[25] For "in this great mortal struggle for honor, freedom, and bread waged by such a creative nation as Germany, no consideration can be shown for impotent, worthless, and overbearing Poles, Czechs, etc. They must be driven to the east, so that the soil becomes free for the tilling by the fists of Germanic peasants" (Alfred Rosenberg, *Myth*, p. 662).

---

25 Translator's note: The quotation in the German does not match the one given in the preceding paragraph (and my translation reflects this incongruity).

Czechs, Poles, and you other "impotent, worthless, and overbearing" nations, listen: You have no right to your land, your states will be wiped off the map of Europe. Everything that Masaryk and Beneš, Pilsudski and Haller, built is to be reduced to rubble in the name of racist theory. Listen, you Poles—and consider whether an alliance with a neighbor who maintains such attitudes can guarantee your security, your future!

Chamberlain and Günther have begun, through racism, to prove the Germans' right to world domination. And today Alfred Rosenberg, the head of the foreign policy office of the ruling party in Germany, has, in his *Myth*, provided the following modest portrayal of the general political situation of the future Great Germany: "Nordic Europe is the slogan of the future, with a German central Europe. Germany as a racial and national state from Strassburg to Memel and beyond, from Eupel to Prague and Laibach, as the central power of the continent..." (*Myth*, p. 629).

The foregoing pages have set out to reveal the origin, nature, goal, and consequences of racism. Anti-Semitism—that "Socialism of fools," as one clever writer has called it—was the intellectual foster father of present-day racism. In witty essays and tomes full of citations, [Arthur de] Gobineau and [Houston Stewart] Chamberlain have paved the way for racism among educated people. With their pseudoscientific books on race that are embellished with photographs, [Hans] Günther and his friends have infested the German youth with racism and prepared them for the brutalism of the Third Reich. From anti-Semitism to racism to brutalism—to the brutal devaluation of one's political and economic adversary, whether that adversary is another party or another people—to the unfettered struggle of all against all, to the scorn for humanity and the victory of animalistic brutality: this is the road that racism is leading humanity down.

In times of serious crisis, anti-Semitism becomes a temptation for politicians. If people are raging against poverty and there are no solutions to be found, then it seems good to have a scapegoat in the Jews, someone to pin the blame on. But anyone who has realized that a direct path leads from anti-Semitism to racism to brutalism will not allow themselves to be tempted by the convenience of anti-Semitic slogans, because that person knows just how dangerous those slogans can be for his own people. All peoples and people groups who were themselves oppressed for centuries must denounce anti-Semitism and fight against it.

Every European should read Hitler's *Mein Kampf* and Rosenberg's *Myth of the 20th Century*. In these books, scorn is preached not only for the Jews. The great French nation as well, which has stood at the forefront of humanity in all its struggles, and which just a few years ago overcame that same Germany in a heroic battle, is insulted and called "degenerate and racially polluted." Vienna, the city of Beethoven and Schubert, is the embodiment of blood defilement according to Hitler. Like the French, the Czechs, Poles, Russians, and so on are dealt with "racially"—because one wants to deal with them politically. The English and Italians are only exempted from the general scorn of all who are different because it is hoped that they can be used as tools.

Racial defamation is supposed to provide the legal basis for the war of aggression. It is supposed to explain to the conquered world that their being robbed and enslaved by the Aryan-Germanic master race is merely a consequence of their racial inferiority, and is an act of justice that is being carried out in the name of the "Myth of the 20th Century."

The poison gas of the chemical factories is supposed to bring to fruition what the intellectual poison gas of racism has ideologically prepared. The peoples who know to protect themselves against armaments with armaments of their own must not forget to defend themselves against intellectual preparations for war as well. There is not much to add to the quotations from *Mein Kampf* and *The Myth of the 20th Century*. These quotations alone demonstrate the danger to the European people, to the whole world. Let us defend ourselves against the intellectual poison gas of racism—before it's too late!

BIBLIOGRAPHY

By Hugo Iltis

From the enormous literature on the problem of race, which only the specialist can today comprehensively review, we are here listing the main works of racism on the one hand, and on the other hand a large number of books that will best help the reader who wants to deepen his study of the race question.

The Main Works of Racism

[Arthur de] Gobineau. *Abhandlung über die Ungleichheit der Menschenrassen* ["An Essay on the Inequality of the Human Races"]. Translated into German by Schemann, 1901.

H.S. Chamberlain. *Die Grundlagen des 19. Jahrhunderts* ["The Foundations of the 19th Century"]. 14th edition, 1929.

H.F.K. Günther. *Rassenkunde des deutschen Volkes* ["Race Theory of the German People"]. Lehmann, Munich, 15th edition, 1930.

H.F.K. Günther. *Rassenkunde des jüdischen Volkes* ["Race Theory of the Jewish People"]. Lehmann, Munich 1930.

Adolf Hitler. *Mein Kampf*. Eher, Munich 1932.

Alfred Rosenberg. *Der Mythus des 20. Jahrhunderts* ["The Myth of the 20th Century"]. Hoheneichen-Verlag, 1932.

A Selection of Important and Interesting Works on the Race Question

Dr. Walter Berger. *Was ist Rasse?* ["What is Race?"]. Vienna, Verlag Gsuhr 1936. A Protestant on the question of race.

Dr. Max Brod. *Rassentheorie und Judentum* ("Race Theory and Judaism"). Prague 1934.

———. *Die Gleichwertigkeit der europäischen Rassen* ("The Equality of the European Races"), the Czech Academy on the Race Question. Prague 1934.

————. *Die Gefährdung des Christentums durch Rassenwahn und Judenverfolgung* ("The Danger Racial Fanaticism and the Persecution of Jews Poses to Christianity"). Vita Nova Verlag, Lucerne 1935.[26]

E.v. Eickstedt. *Rassenkunde und Rassengeschicte der Menschheit* ("Race Theory and Racial History of Humanity"). Enke, Stuttgart 1934. This work, published after Hitler's coup in Germany, provides a large number of facts and pictures, but also of tendentious racist interpretations and fantasies.

Eugen Fischer. *Deutsch Rassenkunde* ("German Race Theory"). G. Fischer, Jena 1929 and ff. The volumes of this great scientific work that were published before Hitler's coup provide the best refutation of racism.

Eugen Fischer. *Die Rehoboter Bastards* ("The Rehoboth Basters"). G. Fischer, Jena 1913.

M. Fishberg. *Die Rassenmerkmale der Juden* ("The Racial Characteristics of the Jews"). Munich 1913.

O. Heller. *Der Untergang des Judentums* ("The Decline of Judaism"). Vienna-Berlin, 2nd edition, 1933.

Dr. Fr. Hertz. *Rasse und Kultur* ("Race and Culture"). A. Kröner, Leipzig, 3rd edition, 1925.

H. Iltis. *Volkstümliche Rassenkunde* ("Popular Race Theory"). Urania, Jena 1930.

H. Iltis. *Rasse in Wissenschaft und Politik* ("Race in Science and Politics"). Urania, Jena 1935 (in Czech).

K. Kautsky. *Rasse und Judentum* ("Race and Judaism"). Stuttgart, 2nd edition, 1922.

Publisher, and responsible for the contents: Rudolf Harand, Vienna 14. Storchengasse 24.
Excerpts and translations only permitted with approval of the publisher.
Printing: Heinrich Gröpner's widow, Vienna 7. Kirchengasse 34.

---

26 Translator's note: This seems to be attributed to Max Brod here in the bibliography, but in the main body text (on page 22 of the German), Iltis notes that this work is by Dr. Desider Bathazar.

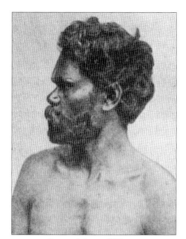

Image 1. Australid Race.
Australian (Queensland). The Australid race is the most primitive human race, and the one closest to prehistoric man.

Image 2. Negrid Race.
A girl from the Negro tribe of the Basuto.
Is the Negro race ugly? (Source: van der Goot.)

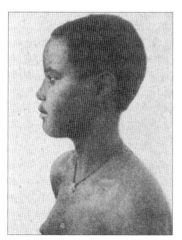

Image 3. Amhara Girl.
The Amhara people in the heart of Abyssinia originated thousands of years ago out of Negrid-Europid miscegenation. The sweetness of the picture is more effective than words at refuting the fables of racial defilement. (Source: M. Grühl.)

Image 4. Abyssinian.
A Negrid-Orientalid racial mixture. A masculinely beautiful, courageous kind of people!
(Source: Osgood.)

Image 5. Mongolid Race.
A Yakut from northern Siberia. (Source: Jochelson.)

Image 6. Mongolid Race.
Sun Yat-sen, Chinese leader and statesman.

Image 7. Nordic Race.
King Frederick William III of Prussia.

Image 8. Nordic-Phalian Race.
General Ludendorff, a leader in the World War.
The racists' view holds that the Nordic race truly
is the most culturally creative.

Image 9. Mediterranean Race.
General Mangin, a leader in the World War.

Image 10. Alpine Race.
Matthias Erzberger, a leader of the Catholic
Center Party, murdered by Nazis.

Image 11. Alpine Race.
Tyrolean child from Ritten. (Source: Günther.)
The Alpine race, to which belongs a large part of the
population of central Germany, Switzlerland, Sudetenland, etc.
is, according to the racists, inferior and lacking in grace.

Image 12. Ostic Race.
Marie von Ebner-Eschenbach, the great German-Austrian
poet. The Ostic race is also, in the view of the racists,
inferior and destined for servitude.

161

Image 13. Dinaric Race.
Jakob Burckhardt, Swiss art historian.
The Dinaric race is closely related to the Armenid race.

Image 14. Dinaric Race.
The Austrian poet Ludwig Anzengruber. The Dinaric race
inhabits the Alps and the Balkans, and continues beyond
the Near East as the Armenid race.

Image 15. Armenid or Near-Eastern Race. Syrian.
The Armenid race, closely related to the Dinaric race,
is a main element of the Jewish mixed race.

Image 16. Armenid Race.
Kemal Pasha "Ataturk," dictator of modern Turkey.

Image 17. J.W. Goethe.
The great German poet. Of mixed race (medium height, brunette, brachycranial, etc.); perhaps a Dinaric-Mediterranean?

Image 18. Martin Luther
The religious reformist and founder of the standard German language. Of mixed race, perhaps Alpine-Ostic? The greatest Germans were racially mixed and often entirely un-Nordic.

Image 19. Ludwig van Beethoven.
Of mixed race, short, stocky, brunette, broad-nosed, etc. Predominantly Alpine. According to Günther, the Alpine race is devoid of all genius. Beethoven's father was psychopathic. Had the sterilization laws of the German Reich already been in place back then, the Ninth Symphony would never have been written.

Image 20. Elisabeth Simon was voted "Miss Hungaria."
It was only after the contest that people found out that this blonde, blue-eyed beauty is a Jew. According to the racists, the Jewish race is a bodily inferior race.

163

Image 21. Max Liebermann.
German-Jewish painter and German-Prussian strategist
(Near Eastern-Orientalid mixed type) in front of the portrait
he painted of Hindenburg (Nordic-Dalic type).

Image 22. The Jewish Mixed Race.
A Jew from Jerusalem.

Image 23. The Jewish Mixed Race.
Joseph Trumpeldor, the leader of the Jewish Legion
at Gallipoli, the organizer of the Jewish land-workers youth
movement (the HeHalutz). Nordic-Armenid type.

Image 24. The Jewish Mixed Race.
(The Armenian element comes to the fore here.)
Sigmund Freud, the brilliant founder of psychoanalysis. He developed a new domain of psychology and the science of the mind. There
are psychoanalytic institutions and journals all over the world.

Image 25. The Jewish Mixed Race.
(The Orientalid element comes to the fore here.)
Julius Tandler, a leading anatomist and social hygienist. Organizer
of the welfare service institutions in Vienna, Greece, China, etc.

Image 26. The Jewish Mixed Race.
(Typical Nordic head.)
Friedrich Gundolf, the great Goethe and Shakespeare
scholar, a leading German literary historian.

Image 27. The Jewish Mixed Race.
(The Alpine element is dominant.)
Alfred Adler, the founder of modern individual psychology,
one of the foundations of modern child-rearing.

Image 28. The True "Aryans."
Indian rajas and maharajas in Delhi 1919. They belong to the Orientalid race, which
also plays a significant role in the Jews.

Image 29. Racial Crossbreed.
A Rehoboth Baster. Source: Eugen Fischer.
Is miscegenation dangerous? A healthy, competent people
emerged from the crossing of Dutch people and Hottentots.

Image 30. R.N. Coudenhove-Kalergi.
The leader of the Paneuropean Movement. His father
is German, his mother Japanese. Is miscegenation
blood defilement?

INDEX

Notes to the Index: For brevity, titles of persons, such as Count, are not given. All text is listed by page number. Notes are listed by page and note number.

Hugo Iltis

Race, Genetics, and Science:
Resisting Racism in the 1930s

Published by Masaryk University,
Žerotínovo nám. 617/9, 601 77 Brno, Czech Republic

Translations by Kareem James Abu-Zeid and Christopher Reid

Edition graphic and cover design / Pavel Křepela
First edition / 2017
Number of copies / 300 cps.
Printing / TISKÁRNA Letovice, Masarykovo nám. 3a, 679 61 Letovice, CZ

ISBN 978-80-210-8764-4